Questions & Answers From the Bible

By
Richard L. Noblit

DEDICATION

To the memory of my parents, Elmer and Myrtle Noblit, and to my wife, Marjorie, whose patience and encouragement helped to make this book possible.

THANK YOU

Rhonda McLaughlin Noblit   Rosie Predmore

Printed by
The Herald Printing Co.
New Washington, Ohio

COPYRIGHT © 2000
BY
RICHARD L. NOBLIT
240 IONA DRIVE
BUCYRUS, OH 44820

Permission was granted to use The King James Bible Reference Edition, copyright 1972 by Thomas Nelson Inc. Camden, New Jersey 08103, to write this book.

TABLE OF CONTENTS

Old Testament	Questions	Answers	New Testament	Questions	Answers
Genesis	3	49	Matthew	87	135
Exodus	5	51	Mark	92	139
Leviticus	7	53	Luke	95	142
Numbers	8	54	John	100	146
Deuteronomy	10	56	The Acts	104	149
Joshua	12	57	Romans	107	151
Judges	13	58	I Corinthians	109	153
Ruth	14	59	II Corinthians	110	154
I Samuel	15	60	Galatians	111	155
II Samuel	16	61	Ephesians	112	156
I Kings	17	62	Philippians	113	157
II Kings	18	63	Colossians	114	158
I Chronicles	19	64	I Thessalonians	115	159
II Chronicles	20	65	II Thessalonians	116	160
Ezra	21	66	I Timothy	117	161
Nehemiah	22	66	II Timothy	118	162
Esther	23	67	Titus	119	162
Job	24	67	Philemon	120	162
Psalms	25	68	Hebrews	121	163
Proverbs	26	68	James	122	164
Ecclesiastes	27	69	I Peter	123	165
Song of Solomon	28	69	II Peter	124	166
Isaiah	29	70	I John	125	167
Jeremiah	30	71	II John	126	168
Lamentations	31	72	III John	127	168
Ezekiel	32	72	Jude	128	168
Daniel	33	73	Revelation	129	169
Hosea	34	75	Questions from the Bible	173	175
Joel	35	75			
Amos	36	76			
Obadiah	37	76			
Jonah	38	77			
Micah	39	77			
Nahum	40	78			
Habakkuk	41	78			
Zephaniah	42	79			
Haggai	43	79			
Zechariah	44	80			
Malachi	45	81			

Old Testament Questions

GENESIS

QUESTIONS:

1. What did God create in the very beginning?
2. God made two great lights. What were they for?
3. In Genesis, 1:27, what did God do on the 6th day of creation?
4. Where did God get the material to make man?
5. What did God plant?
6. A river went out of Eden and parted into four rivers. What were their names?
7. What tree did God tell Adam and Eve not to eat of, but they disobeyed and did anyway?
8. Who named all the animals, birds, and living things on earth?
9. If man was made of dust or dirt, what was woman made of?
10. Who told Eve she could eat anything in the garden?
11. After Adam and Eve ate of the forbidden fruit, they were naked. What did they do when they heard God coming?
12. The LORD God made coats of skins, what for?
13. Did Adam and Eve have children?
14. How many children did Adam and Eve have?
15. What were the children's names that Adam and Eve had?
16. Which son killed his brother?
17. How many years did Adam live?
18. How many years did Seth live?
19. In Chapter 5, Lamech had a son. What was his name?
20. How many sons did Noah and his wife have?
21. What were the names of Noah and his wife's three sons?
22. What did God tell Noah to build?
23. How big was the ark in feet?
24. How long did it rain?
25. How many people were in the ark?
26. How old was Noah when he went in the ark?
27. How long was the water on the earth during the flood?
28. How did God get the water off of the earth?

29. What was the name of the first bird that Noah sent out off the ark to see if there was dry land?

30. What was the name of the second bird that Noah sent out?

31. Did the dove return?

32. After Noah sent the dove out the second time, what did the dove bring back?

33. After the dove brought back the olive leaf, Noah waited seven days and sent the dove out again. Did the dove come back?

34. On the first month and the first day, what did Noah do?

35. When all living things left the ark, what did Noah build?

36. After the altar was built, the flood was over, and the ground was dry, what did the Lord say to himself?

37. What did God say to Noah and his family after the flood?

38. God said we can eat the meat of animals, but what part of the animal should we not eat?

39. "Whoso sheddeth man's blood..." what did God say would happen to them?

40. In 9:7, what does God tell us to do?

41. What did God mean when he said he would establish his covenant with us?

42. What sign does God put in the sky that there will never be another flood?

43. Which one of Noah's sons was the father of Canaan?

44. What did Noah plant?

45. How did Noah get drunk?

46. How long did Noah live after the flood?

47. How many total years did Noah live?

EXODUS

QUESTIONS:

1. Who was the new king that rose up in Egypt?
2. What did the Egyptians make the children of Israel do?
3. What did the king of Egypt tell the Hebrew midwives to do when there was a baby boy born?
4. Did the midwives kill the baby boys?
5. What did Pharaoh tell all of his people to do with their baby boys?
6. What was Moses' mother's name?
7. Who gave Moses his name?
8. Why did Pharaoh want to kill Moses? (Ex. 2-12)
9. What was Moses' wife's name?
10. God spoke to Moses out of a burning bush. What did he say to him?
11. What did Moses do when he was standing on the holy ground, and God said, "I am the God of thy father, the God of Abraham, the God of Isaac, and the God of Jacob. And Moses..." what?
12. Where did God want Moses to go when Moses said to God, "...I am slow of speech, and of a slow tongue"?
13. Who did Moses take along to Egypt?
14. Who said in Exodus, "...I know not the Lord, neither will I let Israel go."?
15. Moses had a brother. What was his name?
16. When God asked Moses and Aaron to bring the children of Israel out of Egypt, how old were they?
17. In the 7th chapter, when they tell the age of Aaron and Moses, how many years is a score?
18. God speaks of a predator and two kinds of insects in chapter 8. What are they?
19. When Pharaoh would not let the Israelites go out of Egypt, what animals were involved?
20. What insect is mentioned that will haunt all of Egypt?
21. How did God bring the locusts into Egypt?
22. In chapter 12, what animal did they kill?
23. How long were the children of Israel in Egypt?
24. Why did the Egyptians want the children of Israel to stay in Egypt?
25. What happened when the Lord told Moses to lift up his hand over the sea?
26. What happened to Pharaoh and his army, his chariots, his horses, and the other people that went in the dry sea after the Israelites?

27. What was the name of the sea that Pharaoh and his chariots drowned in?

28. In 16:16, God speaks of the word omer. What is an omer?

29. Why did the people gather twice as much omer on the sixth day?

30. In the 16th chapter, "And Moses said unto Aaron, Take a pot, and put an omer full of manna therein, and lay it up before the LORD, to be kept for your generations." What is manna?

31. After the people of Israel came out of the wilderness, they got thirsty. What did God tell Moses to strike to get water?

32. Who was Moses' father-in-law?

33. What would happen to the people if they went up Mount Sinai or touched it?

34. Where are the Ten Commandments found in the Bible?

35. After the commandments were recorded, God asked Moses to build an altar. What kind of material did God tell Moses to use?

36. What chapter are the judgments found in?

37. If you strike your father or mother, what could happen to you?

38. How many elders were in Moses' tribe?

39. How many tribes were in Israel?

40. In what chapter does God give Moses the law and commandments to be recorded?

41. In Genesis 7:4, it speaks of forty days and forty nights. Where in Exodus does the Bible speak of forty days and forty nights?

42. God told Moses to tell his people they should willingly bring him an offering. What was the offering?

43. In Exodus, in which chapter is gold mentioned sixteen times?

44. How many curtains did God tell the people to make for the tabernacle?

45. What kinds of metal are mentioned in chapter 26?

46. What is shittim wood?

47. In chapter 28, what kind of garments did God tell the people of Israel to make for Aaron?

48. What is a shekel?

49. How many times is shekel mentioned in chapter 30?

50. In chapter 31, what does God strongly tell us to do? If we do not, "...he shall surely be put to death."

51. What book of the Bible is after Exodus?

LEVITICUS

QUESTIONS:

1. In chapter one, verse one, where was the Lord when he spoke to Moses?
2. The Lord suggested to Moses that the people of Israel should bring three kinds of animals to the altar. What were they?
3. There are seven kinds of food named in chapter two. What are they?
4. God told Moses to tell the people of Israel when they bring an animal for an offering to the Lord, what should this animal be?
5. In Leviticus, chapter three, last verse, the Lord tells the priest what two parts of the animal they should not eat. What are they?
6. In chapter four, what animals did the Lord tell Moses to tell the people of Israel to bring to the door of the tabernacle and kill it before the Lord?
7. How many times is "bullock" said in Leviticus, chapter four?
8. What is a trespass offering?
9. In chapter twelve, it speaks of the separation of boy babies being forty days. How many days was it for girl babies?
10. What was the most dreaded diseases in Moses' and Aaron's days before the flood?
11. Who determined who had leprosy and what should be done with them?
12. If an entire household has leprosy, what will the priest do with it?
13. In Leviticus, chapter sixteen, who died?
14. In chapter sixteen, where did the scapegoat go?
15. What country, that was Israel's neighbors, was very wicked?
16. In chapter nineteen and twenty, there are at least twenty-two different types of sins committed. Name ten of them.
17. In chapter twenty-five, what did God tell Moses to tell the people of Israel to do with the land?
18. What is a Jubilee year?
19. The number "seven" comes up very often throughout the Bible. What are some of them? (Like every 7th day, a Sabbath.)
20. What is the next chapter after Leviticus?

NUMBERS

QUESTIONS:

1. In chapter 1, what was the first census taken for?

2. Why was this census so important?

3. There were fourteen tribes in the wilderness after they came out of Egypt. Who were the leaders of these tribes?

4. How many men were in Reuben's camp?

5. What tribe did God tell Moses to care for the tabernacle?

6. When the census was taken on Mt. Sinai, of all the tribes, how many men were over 20 years of age?

7. In chapter 4, Aaron and his sons will cover the ark of testimony with blue cloth and with what other covering?

8. In chapter 5 are the words ephah of barley meal. How much would ephah be in U.S. measure?

9. In chapter 6, what animals were there when the Nazarite's days were fulfilled?

10. Chapter 6:24-26 says, the Lord said to Aaron to bless the children of Israel. What did He say?

11. When Moses set up the tabernacle and anointed and sanctified it, the princes of the tribes brought their offering before the Lord. How did they bring their offering to the Lord?

12. In chapter 7, when the princes of Israel had dedication of the altar and it was anointed—how many oxen were given as peace offerings?

13. The Lord told Moses, "Take the Levites from among the children of Israel, and..." what?

14. When a cloud covered the tabernacle, what did it appear to look like at night?

15. When the cloud went off the tabernacle, where did it go?

16. Who led the march to the Promised Land?

17. Where were the children of Israel marching to?

18. What was the name of the woman that complained against Moses?

19. What disease did Miriam get?

20. How many spies did Moses send out to spy on Canaan?

21. Did the people of Israel ever get to Canaan?

22. There were two men out of the 600,000 men over twenty lived to enter Canaan. Who were they?

23. What was the man's name that rose up against Moses?

24. Moses sin cost him the Promised Land. What was that sin?

25. Miriam, Aaron and Moses all died in the same year. Where did each one die?

26. Where did the book of Numbers get its name?

27. On the Jewish calendar, there was a sacred year and a civil year. What time in the year did they start?

28. In chapter 31, there are six kinds of metals mentioned. What are they?

29. How old was Aaron when he died?

30. How many years was it from the time the children of Israel came out of Egypt and the Lord commanded Aaron to go to Mount Hor? (He died there.)

31. How old were Miriam and Moses when they died?

32. What is the next chapter after Numbers?

DEUTERONOMY

QUESTIONS:

1. What does the word Deuteronomy mean?

2. In chapter 1, God told the people, "Behold, I have set the land before you: go in and possess the land which the LORD sware unto you fathers..." Who were these three fathers?

3. 5:3 says, "And Moses called all Israel, and said unto them, Hear, O Israel, the statutes and judgments which I speak in your ears this day, that ye may learn them, and keep, and do them." What are the statutes and judgments they should keep?

4. What other book in the Bible has the Ten Commandments?

5. What did God write the Ten Commandments on?

6. Who did God give the Commandments to?

7. In chapter 4 and 5, it is said many times: "out of the midst of the fire;" or "his great fire;" and "the mountain did burn with fire." What did the Lord mean by this?

8. What is the great commandment? It is said many times throughout the Bible. Jesus said it in Matthew 22:37.

9. In chapter 6, what did God command us as parents, teachers, and all adults to teach our children?

10. What did God call the people of Israel when they were so rebellious against him?

11. In chapter 11, God showed his greatness, his mighty hand, and his stretched out arm. What were the miracles he did?

12. In chapter 16, three times a year all the males were required to appear before God. What were these great feasts called?

13. In chapter 19, Moses set aside three cities for those people who had caused accidental death to hide in. What were the three cities?

14. In chapter 20, before the men went into battle, the priest gave four reasons that men could be excused from military service. What were the four reasons?

15. In chapter 22:5, it is a sin if we don't wear the right kind of clothes. What does God tell us to do?

16. In chapter 27, what material were the curses at Mount Ebal written on?

17. How many curses were there at Mount Ebal?

18. What nation's army was the Lord talking about when he told the Hebrews that he would send an army as swift as the flying eagle?

19. In both the Babylonian and Roman sieges of Jerusalem, what did parents do to their children?

20. Moses' last words to Israel, while they were in the land of Moab, were to choose as to how they were to serve God. What were their two choices?

21. In chapter 31, how old was Moses the day he spoke to Israel?

22. In chapter 31, the Lord said to Moses that it was time for him to die. Who succeeded him?

23. Moses composed several songs before his death; one of those is a Psalm. Which Psalm is it?

24. Where did Moses die?

25. What book follows Deuteronomy?

JOSHUA

QUESTIONS:

1. Who was Joshua's father?
2. God gave Joshua a solemn warning when he was going to Jericho and Gilgal. This warning is repeated four times in chapter one. What is the warning?
3. What was the woman's name who hid the two spies in chapter two?
4. In chapter four there were twelve stones put at two different places as a memorial yet today. Where are the two places?
5. When the children of Israel camped in Gilgal, what did they celebrate?
6. Jericho is about six miles from the Jordan River. How far is Gilgal from the Jordan River?
7. How many acres were inside the wall of Jericho?
8. What happened to the great wall of Jericho?
9. How many walls were there?
10. After the walls were destroyed, what then did they do to the city of Jericho?
11. When Joshua and his men left Jericho, how many soldiers did Joshua take to invade and capture Ai?
12. After Joshua and his men captured Ai, what did they do to the city?
13. What did they do to the King of Ai?
14. The Amorites consist of five kings and their country. What are their names?
15. What does it mean, "The battle where the sun stood still"?
16. What happened to the five kings after Joshua's men defeated them?
17. How many kings were killed when Joshua and his men conquered their land?
18. What did Joshua, in his later days, tell his people to beware of?
19. How old was Joshua when he died?
20. Where did they bury Joshua?
21. What book is after Joshua?

JUDGES

QUESTIONS:

1. After Joshua died, whom did God appoint after him?
2. Who was Judah's brother?
3. What did Judah and Simeon do to Adonibezek?
4. What did the children of Israel do in chapter 2:12 to provoke God?
5. In chapter 2, what did the Lord raise up to help Israel?
6. After Sisera was defeated in chapter 4, he ran from his chariot and hid in Jael's tent, the wife of Heber. What did she do to him?
7. The number 40 is used throughout the Bible a number of times. Name eight of those times.
8. In chapter 6, who said he was an angel of the Lord?
9. Who did the Lord say, "...Peace be unto thee; fear not: thou shalt not die."
10. The Lord told Gideon to build an altar. Gideon took ten men servants, and built the altar at night. Why did they build the altar at night?
11. Who was Gideon's father?
12. In chapter 8, how many men were with Gideon when he invaded the Midianites, Amalekites, and the Arabians?
13. How many men did Gideon and his men kill?
14. Israel wanted Gideon and his son to rule over them. What did Gideon tell them?
15. Gideon said that he would like a request and that he wanted the men of Israel to put all of their earrings of gold put on a blanket. How many pounds of gold were there?
16. In chapter 15, Samson caught three hundred foxes and set them on fire. What else did he set on fire?
17. Samson found a jawbone of a colt. What did he do with it?
18. How many years did Samson judge Israel?
19. How did Samson die?
20. Who was the last of the Judges mentioned in the book of Judges?
21. What book follows the book of Judges?

RUTH

QUESTIONS:

1. Ruth was the great grandmother of what great king?

2. How long was Ruth married the first time?

3. In the first chapter, what is the name of another woman that is named in the chapter? She was married eight years.

4. When Naomi and Ruth left the country of Moab and returned to Bethlehem, what grain was ready to be harvested?

5. Who was Ruth's mother-in-law?

6. Ruth was the great grandmother of a popular king. Who was that king?

7. In whose field did Ruth glean corn?

8. Boaz and Ruth got married and had a son. What was his name?

9. What book of the Bible is after Ruth?

I SAMUEL

QUESTIONS:

1. Where was Samuel born?
2. Samuel had two offices. Where were they?
3. Who was Samuel's mother?
4. How many children did Hannah have?
5. In chapter three, how many times did the Lord call to Samuel for him to come to him?
6. Who did Samuel replace as judge?
7. How many men were killed in chapter four?
8. When the Philistines fought Israel, the two sons of Eli were killed. What happened to Eli when he heard they were killed?
9. How old was Eli when he died?
10. In chapter 7, what did Samuel offer unto the Lord to protect Israel from the Philistines?
11. "And Samuel judged Israel all the days of his life." What three places or towns did he visit regularly?
12. In chapter eleven, in what town did Samuel and the people of Israel go to make Saul king of Israel?
13. In chapter 12, on a day of wheat harvest, what did the Lord do that day to stop the harvest?
14. In chapter 13, Samuel said to Saul that he did something foolishly. What was the foolish thing he did?
15. Saul made a mistake in chapter 13, in chapter 14, and in chapter 15. What were the three mistakes made?
16. Who became Saul's armor-bearer?
17. David killed two animals in chapter 17. What were they?
18. How many stones did David pick up out of the brook and put in his shepherd's bag when he went to kill Goliath?
19. After David hit Goliath in the forehead with a stone, and after Goliath fell on his face, what did David do to him?
20. What did David do with Goliath's head?
21. How tall was Goliath?
22. How did Saul die?
23. What book follows I Samuel?

II SAMUEL

QUESTIONS:

1. In chapter 2, who killed Asahel?

2. Where on Asahel's body did Abner hit him with his spear?

3. In chapter 11, whom did David write a letter to?

4. David and his wife, Bathsheba had a son. What was his name?

5. What did Absalom tell his servants to do to Joab's field of barley?

6. In chapter 17, Ahithophel killed himself. What method did he use?

7. In chapter 18, how many men were killed in the battle of the servants of David and the people of Israel?

8. How did Absalom, the king's son, get killed?

9. In chapter 20, whom did Joab kill?

10. In chapter 21, how many fingers and toes did the son of the giant have?

11. How many sons did the giant Gath have?

12. Who said, "The God of my rock; in him will I trust: he is my shield, and the horn of my salvation, my high tower, and my refuge, my saviour; thou savest me from violence."

13. In what chapter of II Samuel did David say, "When the waves of death compassed me, the floods of ungodly men made me afraid."

14. What were the three things that the Lord offered David, and he was to choose one of them? (Chapter 24)

15. Which one of the three was chosen? David put the decision up to the Lord.

16. What did David buy to build an altar on?

17. What were David's two great accomplishments?

18. What book of the Bible is after II Samuel?

I KINGS

QUESTIONS:

1. When King David was cold, what did his servants put on him to try to keep him warm?
2. After clothes could not warm the King, what did the servants do to try and warm him?
3. What was the girl's name that got to warm the King?
4. Bathsheba had a son. What was his name?
5. When Solomon went to Gihon he rode a mule. Who owned the mule?
6. Who became king of Israel after King David?
7. When David was about to die, what did he tell his son, Solomon, who was going to take his place as king?
8. When David died, where was he buried?
9. How many years did David reign over Israel?
10. Who killed Joab?
11. What country was Pharaoh king of?
12. Solomon went to Gibeon to sacrifice burnt offerings upon the altar. How many did he offer?
13. When Solomon awoke from a dream, "Then came there two women, that were harlots, unto the king, and stood before him." What are harlots?
14. How many horses did Solomon have?
15. In chapter 6, what did Solomon build?
16. What was the main kind of wood used in building the temple?
17. When the temple was finished, Solomon overlaid the entire temple inside and out with what?
18. How many years did it take Solomon to build the temple?
19. Pharaoh, King of Egypt, had a daughter. Who was her husband?
20. King Solomon had a Navy with ships. On what sea did he keep the ships?
21. Solomon loved many strong women besides his wife. How many wives did he have?
22. How many years did Solomon reign over Israel?
23. Where is Solomon buried?
24. After King Solomon died, who took his place as King of Israel?
25. How many years did Jeroboam reign over Israel?
26. Rehoboam, the son of Solomon, reigned in Judah. How many years did he reign in Jerusalem?
27. In chapter 19, Elisha was plowing with twelve yoke of oxen. How many animals would that be?
28. How many years were there without war between Syria and Israel? 22:1
29. In chapter 22, who is the king of Judah?
30. How did Ahab, the king of Israel, get killed?
31. How many chapters are there in 1 Kings?
32. What book follows 1 Kings?

II KINGS

QUESTIONS:

1. What was the man's name that "...He was an hairy man, and girt with a girdle of leather about his loins...."?

2. Elijah was sitting on top of a hill when the king sent a captain and fifty men. The captain said to Elijah, "...Come down...", and Elijah said to the captain, "...If I be a man of God, then let fire come down from heaven..." What did the fire do?

3. In chapter two, there appeared a chariot of fire, and horses of fire. What happened to Elijah?

4. When Elijah went up to heaven, what fell from him?

5. "And he went up from thence unto Bethel: and as he was going up by the way, there came forth little children out of the city, and mocked him and said unto him..." what?

6. What happened to the little children that came out of the city and mocked Elisha?

7. Naaman was captain of the army of Syria. What disease did he have?

8. In chapter 5 Naaman, the captain of the Syria army had leprosy. How did he cure his leprosy?

9. In what chapter and verse are the words, "...as white as snow."?

10. In chapter nine what was the woman's name that the dogs ate her flesh?

11. How many sons did Ahab have?

12. What happened to the seventy sons of the king?

13. What country was Nebuchadnezzar king of?

14. What book is after II Kings?

I CHRONICLES

QUESTIONS:

1. In the book of I Chronicles, what word is mentioned at least eighty times?

2. In Chapter 10, how did Saul die?

3. In Chapter 15, what was King David doing that made Michal, the Daughter of Saul, despise him.

4. When God speaks and says, "For all the gods of the people..." what?

5. There was a man in Gath that was the son of a giant. How many toes and fingers did he have?

6. What is a threshing floor?

7. Who was Solomon's father?

8. What is shewbread?

9. In Chapter 27, how many captains are there?

10. What book is after I Chronicles?

II CHRONICLES

QUESTIONS:

1. Who was Solomon's father?

2. When Solomon became king he asked God for two things. What were they?

3. What were the first two things that Solomon gathered when he became king of Israel?

4. In chapter two, there are three kings of trees mentioned. What are their names?

5. Where did Solomon build the house of the Lord?

6. In chapter nine, what was the footstool made of?

7. What king passed all the kings in riches and wisdom?

8. How long did Solomon reign in Jerusalem and over Israel?

9. Who took Solomon's place as king of Israel?

10. In chapter 18, what time of day did Ahab the king of Israel die?

11. How long did Jehoshaphat reign over Judah?

12. Where is Jehoshaphat buried?

13. When Jehoiada died, how old was he?

14. What city is called the city of palm trees?

15. What book is after II Chronicles?

EZRA

QUESTIONS:

1. What country was Cyrus king of?

2. What country was Nebuchadnezzar king of?

3. In what chapter of Ezra is the words, "The children of," said at least ninety-six times?

4. What was Ezra's title or profession in his time?

5. In chapter 8, what verse says, "...The hand of our God is upon all them for good that seek him; but his power and his wrath is against all them that forsake him."?

6. What book follows the book of Ezra?

NEHEMIAH

QUESTIONS:

1. What happened to the gates of Jerusalem?

2. In chapter 3 there is a word that is used 35 times. What is that word?

3. In chapter 8, what did all the people do when Ezra opened the book?

4. When Ezra blessed the Lord in front of all the people, what did the people do and say?

5. In what country was Solomon king of?

6. What book is after Nehemiah?

ESTHER

QUESTIONS:

1. In chapter 1, the pavement was four different colors. What were the four colors?

2. In chapter 2, were Esther's parents living or dead?

3. When Esther was brought before the king, did she please him?

4. Who was king Ahasuerus's favorite woman?

5. In chapter 7, Haman built gallows to hang Mordecai. How did King Ahasuerus order him to be hanged on the gallows that Haman built?

6. Haman had ten sons. What did Esther ask the king to do with them?

7. What happened to King Ahasuerus and his sons?

8. Who were the two people that ended up being the heroes of the book of Esther?

9. What book follows Esther?

10. Who succeeded King Ahasuerus?

JOB

QUESTIONS:

1. How many children did Job have?

2. When Satan left the presence of the Lord, what did Satan do to Job from his foot to his head?

3. In chapter 16, what kind of cloth was sewed upon his skin?

4. How old was Job when he died?

5. What book is after Job?

PSALMS

QUESTIONS:

1. In Psalm 19 verse 1, "The heavens declare the glory of God; and the firmament sheweth his..." what?

2. In Psalm 20. "Some trust in chariots, and some in horses: but we will remember the name of the..." what three words?

3. What were the words Jesus spoke when he was hanging on the cross? Psalm 22.

4. What is the first verse of Psalm 23?

5. In Psalm 53 verse 1, "The fool hath said in his heart, There is no..." what?

6. Fill in the blank. "The righteous shall rejoice when he seeth vengeance: he shall wash his feet in the _____ of the wicked."

7. How many Psalms or chapters are in the book of Psalms?

8. What is the shortest Psalm in the book of Psalms?

9. What is the longest Psalm or chapter in the Book of Psalms?

10. What book is after the Book of Psalms?

PROVERBS

QUESTIONS:

1. In chapter 7, "I have decked my bed with coverings of tapestry, with carved works, with fine linen of..." what country?

2. "The fear of the LORD is the beginning of..." what?

3. "...A wise son maketh a glad father: but a foolish son is the heaviness of his..." what?

4. "The memory of the just is blessed: but the name of the wicked shall..." what?

5. "A faithful witness will not lie: but a false witness will utter..." what?

6. "Train up a child in the way he should go: and when he is old, he will not..." what?

7. "There are three things that are never satisfied, yea, four things say not, It is enough." Three of the four are, "The grave; and the barren womb; the earth that is not filled with water; and the..." what?

8. What is the book after Proverbs?

ECCLESIASTES

QUESTIONS:

1. In chapter 3, the first verse says, "To every thing there is a season, and a time to every purpose under the heaven:" The second verse says, "A time to be born, and a time to..." what?

2. The fourth verse says, "A time to weep, and a time to..." what?

3. The fifth verse says, "...a time to embrace, and a time to refrain from..." what?

4. The seventh verse says, "...a time to keep silence, and a time to..." what?

5. Verse twenty says, "All go unto one place; all are of the dust, and all turn to..." what?

6. In chapter 7, the first verse says, "A GOOD name is better than precious ointment; and the day of death than the day of one's..." what?

7. Chapter 9, verse 5 says, "For the living know that they shall die: but the dead know not any thing, neither have they any more a reward; for the memory of them is..." what?

8. "Or ever the silver cord be loosed, or the golden bowl be broken, or the pitcher be broken at the..." where?

9. What book is after Ecclesiastes?

SONG OF SOLOMON

QUESTIONS:

1. Who is the Song of Solomon?

2. Verse 5 says, "I am black, but comely,..." Verse 6 says, "Look not upon me, because I am black..." How did he get black?

3. In chapter 1, what color is the bed?

4. King Solomon made himself something out of wood from Lebanon, what was it?

5. What did every one of the flocks of sheep bear?

6. How many chapters are in the Song of Solomon?

7. What book is after the Song of Solomon?

ISAIAH

QUESTIONS:

1. In chapter 1, what does it say about the head and heart?

2. Who was Isaiah's father?

3. When it was said, "...and they will beat their swords into..." what?

4. In chapter 6, how many wings did each seraphim have?

5. "...Behold, a virgin shall conceive, and bear a son, and shall call his name..." what?

6. In chapter 7, there are three foods talked about. Two of them are butter and milk. What is the third one?

7. Chapter 22 verse 7 says, "And it shall come to pass, that they choicest valleys shall be full of..." what?

8. "And he shall break it as the breaking of the potters' vessel that is..." what?

9. Fill in the blanks. "For the _____ is our judge, the _____ is our lawgiver, the _____ is our king; he will save us."

10. What language was used in chapter 36? It was not Jewish.

11. What kind of trees were cut down? There were two.

12. In chapter 54, "...for as I have sworn that the waters of Noah should no more go over..." what?

13. In chapter 55, what two things can you buy without money?

14. What is a cockatrice egg?

15. In the last chapter of Isaiah, what verse says, "For as the new heavens and the new earth, which I will make, shall remain before me, saith the LORD, so shall your seed and your name remain."?

16. How many chapters are in Isaiah?

17. What book comes after Isaiah?

JEREMIAH

QUESTIONS:

1. What country did the Lord say was backsliding?

2. In chapter 4, what musical instrument sounds?

3. Who gathers the wood in chapter 7?

4. In chapter 10, verse 9, the Lord is speaking to Israel. What color were the two pieces of clothing?

5. Which disciple killed himself in despair?

6. Who was king of Babylon in chapter 22?

7. Chapter 28 verse 14 says, "...I have put a yoke of iron upon the neck of all these..." what?

8. In chapter 32, verse 17, what did God make with His great power?

9. In chapter 38, the princes wanted Jeremiah put to death. Where did they put him to die?

10. Who burned the king's house and broke down the walls of Jerusalem? What group of people?

11. God punished Jerusalem three different ways. Name two of them?

12. "Babylon hath been a golden cup in the LORD'S hand, that made all the earth drunken: the nations have drunken of her wine; therefore the nations are mad." What happened to Babylon?

13. "...The daughter of Babylon is like a..." what?

14. In chapter 52, verse 14, what did the Chaldeans do to Jerusalem?

15. How many chapters are in the book of Jeremiah?

16. What book follows Jeremiah?

LAMENTATIONS

QUESTIONS:

1. "From above hath he sent fire into my..." what?

2. In chapter 2, verse 18, "Their heart cried unto the Lord, O wall of the daughter of Zion, let tears run down like a..." what?

3. "The LORD is good unto them that..." what?

4. How many chapters are in the book of Lamentations?

5. What book follows Lamentations?

EZEKIEL

QUESTIONS:

1. "Also out of the midst thereof came the likeness of four living creatures. And this was their appearance; they had the likeness of a man." What two features did they possess?

2. Chapter 14 verse 6 says, "...Repent, and turn yourselves from your..." what?

3. What 3 famous men's names are told in chapter 14 verse 14?

4. "The soul that sinneth, it shall..." what?

5. In chapter 22 verse 18, there are 5 medals. What are they?

6. What does the word dross mean in chapter 22?

7. What are the three kinds of trees mentioned in chapter 27?

8. How many years did God say He would make the land of Egypt desolate?

9. In chapter 32 verse 7, what did God say He would cover the sun with?

10. In chapter 21 it is said many times, "slain by" what?

11. In chapter 40, there is a word that is used over forty times and another is used over thirty-five times. What are they?

12. In chapter 45, the word homer is mentioned. How many bushels are in a homer?

13. Fill in the blanks. "...The gate of the inner court that looketh toward the east shall be shut the six working days; but on the _____ it shall be opened, and in the day of the _____ it shall be opened."

14. What book follows Ezekiel?

DANIEL

QUESTIONS:

1. In what city was Daniel's ministry?
2. Before Christian time, who was Daniel's friend?
3. Where was Daniel born?
4. Who in chapter 2 dreamed dreams?
5. Who were the four children of God in chapter one?
6. What was Nebuchadnezzar's dream?
7. From the days of Daniel to the coming of Christ, who were the four world empires? These four empires ruled the world in that time period.
8. How large was the head of gold that Nebuchadnezzar had made?
9. What three men did Nebuchadnezzar have punished by his strongest army men? What did the army men do to them?
10. What year did Nebuchadnezzar burn Jerusalem?
11. In chapter 4, Nebuchadnezzar had a dream that made him afraid. What was this dream?
12. In chapter 5, who was made the third ruler in the kingdom by proclamation?
13. How many years was Daniel in the Babylonian Empire?
14. Daniel had a position directly below King Darius. What one thing did Daniel do and say that led up to him being thrown in the lions' den?
15. Did the lions kill Daniel?
16. What one thing was the downfall of Nebuchadnezzar and Darius?
17. King Darius had all the men that accused Daniel of worshipping his God to be thrown in the lions' den. What happened to them?
18. In chapter 7, Daniel had a dream and vision. What animals did he see?
19. Since the Roman Empire, there have been three men that tried to rule the world. Who were they?
20. Who was the King of Persia?
21. In chapter 10, Daniel had a great vision. What was that vision?
22. In chapter 11, what empires are south and north?
23. The king of the south invaded the king of the north. Which one won the battle?
24. What things and happenings are taking place in our time to tell us the end of time is near?
25. In chapter 12, what did God mean when he told Daniel to "Go thy way"?
26. What book follows Daniel?

HOSEA

QUESTIONS:

1. Who was Jeroboam's father?

2. What was Hosea's wives name?

3. In chapter 4, there are five commandments that are broken. They are swearing, lying, killing, stealing, and committing adultery. Which commandments are these? Ex., swearing is the 2nd Commandment.

4. What kind of a bird is called "silly" in chapter 7?

5. In chapter 12, what country did Jacob flee into?

6. How many chapters are in the book of Hosea?

7. What is the book after Hosea?

JOEL

QUESTIONS:

1. There are four bugs or insects mentioned in chapter one. What are they?

2. Fill in the blanks. "For a nation is come up upon my land, strong, and without number, whose teeth are the teeth of a _____, and he hath the cheek teeth of a great _____. "What kind of an animal does the teeth belong to in chapter 1, verse 6?

3. In chapter two, what musical instrument was blown?

4. In verse ten, "The earth shall quake before them; the heavens shall tremble: the sun and the moon shall be dark, and the stars shall..." what?

5. Fill in the blanks. "Be glad then, ye children of Zion, and rejoice in the LORD your God: for he hath given you the _____ rain moderately, and he will cause to come down for you the _____, the _____ rain, and the _____ rain in the first month."

6. Verse 31 says, "The sun shall be turned into darkness, and the moon into..." what?

7. In chapter three, verse three, a girl was sold for a drink. What was the drink?

8. Fill in the blanks. "Beat your plowshares into _____ and your pruninghooks into _____: let the weak say, I am strong."

9. "Let the heathen be wakened, and come up to the valley of..." what valley?

10. What are the three liquids mentioned in chapter three verse eighteen? They are very common in our day.

11. How many chapters are in Joel?

12. What book is after Joel?

AMOS

QUESTIONS:

1. What two kinds of trees are named in chapter two, verse nine?

2. In chapter five, verse fifteen, it says, "Hate the evil, and love..." what?

3. "And the LORD said unto me, Amos, what seest thou?" What did Amos see?

4. What did Amos say would happen to Jeroboam, the king of Israel? "For thus Amos saith, Jeroboam shall die by the..." what?

5. "And it shall come to pass in that day, saith the Lord GOD, that I will cause the sun to go down at noon, and I will..." what?

6. "Behold, the days come, saith the Lord GOD, that I will send a famine in the land, not a famine of bread, nor a thirst for water, but of..." what?

7. In chapter nine, "...the mountains shall drop sweet wine, and all the hills shall..." what?

8. How many chapters are in the book of Amos?

9. What book follows Amos?

OBADIAH

QUESTIONS:

1. In verse one, "...we have heard a rumor from the LORD, and an ambassador is sent among the..." what kind of people?

2. What would the grape-gatherers leave in the fields?

3. How many chapters are in the book of Obadiah?

4. What book is after Obadiah?

JONAH

QUESTIONS:

1. "But the LORD sent out a great _____ into the sea, and there was a mighty _____ in the sea, so that the ship was like to be broken"?

2. What did Jonah do when he went down inside the ship?

3. What nationality was Jonah?

4. When Jonah was cast into the sea, what happened to him?

5. How long was Jonah in the belly of the great fish?

6. What did Jonah do while in the fish's belly?

7. How did Jonah get out of the big fish?

8. After Jonah was vomited out of the big fish, what city did the Lord tell Jonah to go and preach?

9. In chapter three, what kind of clothes did the people put on? Even the king took off his robe and put on the same thing.

10. How many chapters are in Jonah?

11. What is the book that follows Jonah?

MICAH

QUESTIONS:

1. In chapter three, verse two, "Who hate the good, and love..." who?
2. Fill in the blanks. "And he shall judge among many people, and rebuke strong nations afar off; and they shall beat their swords into _____, and their spears into _____: nation shall not lift up a sword against nation, neither shall they learn war any more."
3. In 6:6 it says, "Wherewith shall I come before the LORD, and bow myself before the high God? Shall I come before him with burnt offerings, with calves of a..." How old were the calves?
4. In chapter six, verse fifteen, "Thou shalt sow, but thou shalt not..." what?
5. "For the son dishonoureth the father, the daughter riseth up against her..." who?
6. How many chapters are in the book of Micah?
7. What book follows Micah?

NAHUM

QUESTIONS:

1. "He rebuketh the sea, and maketh it..." what?

2. What does He do to all the rivers?

3. "The shield of his mighty men is made of..." what color?

4. In chapter two, verse four, what do the chariots seem like?

5. What two countries are mentioned in chapter three verse nine?

6. How many chapters are in the book of Nahum?

7. What book follows Nahum?

HABAKKUK

QUESTIONS:

1. In chapter two verse nineteen, "Woe unto him that saith to the wood..." what does it say to the wood?

2. What does it say to the dumb stone?

3. In verse twenty, "But the LORD is in his holy..." what place?

4. In chapter three verse two it says, "O Lord, I have heard thy speech and was..." what?

5. How many chapters are in the book of Habakkuk?

6. What book is after Habakkuk?

ZEPHANIAH

QUESTIONS:

1. "I will consume man and beast; I will consume the fowls of the heaven, and the fishes of the..." what?

2. "...I will punish the princes, and the king's children, and all such as are clothed with strange..." what?

3. "...they shall also build houses, but not..." what?

4. "That day is a day of wrath, a day of trouble and distress, a day of wasteness and desolation, a day of darkness and gloominess, a day of clouds and thick..." what?

5. "...because they have sinned against the LORD: and their blood shall be poured out as dust, and their flesh as the..." what?

6. Fill in the blanks. "Neither their _____ nor their _____ shall be able to deliver them in the day of the LORDS'S _____; but the whole land shall be devoured by the _____ of his jealousy: for he shall make even a speedy riddance of all them that _____ in the land."

7. "Therefore as I live, said the LORD of hosts, the God of Israel, Surely Moab shall be as Sodom, and the children of Ammon as..." what?

8. Fill in the blank. "...for he shall uncover the _____ work." What is the name of the wood?

9. In chapter three verse three, "Her princes within her are roaring..." what?

10. "...for all the earth shall be devoured with the fire of my..." what?

11. Fill in the blank. "From beyond the rivers of _____ my suppliants, even the daughter of my dispersed, shall bring mine offering."

12. "Sing, O daughter of Zion; shout, O Israel; be glad and rejoice with all the heart O daughter of..." what town?

13. How many chapters are in the book of Zephaniah?

14. What book is after Zephaniah?

HAGGAI

QUESTIONS:

1. Was Haggai a prophet?

2. "...he that earneth wages earneth wages to put it into a bag with..." what?

3. "Go up to the mountain, and bring wood, and build the..." what?

4. What prophet is mentioned in chapter one verse twelve?

5. "For thus saith the LORD of hosts; Yet once, it is a little while, and I will shake the heavens, and the earth, and the sea, and the..." what?

6. "And again the word of the LORD came unto..." who?

7. How many chapters are in Haggai?

8. What book is after Haggai?

ZECHARIAH

QUESTIONS:

1. The Lord said, "...Turn ye now from your..." what?

2. "I saw by night, and behold a man riding upon a..." what color of horse?

3. In chapter one verse ten, what kind of trees was the man standing among? It is my mother's first name?

4. "Now Joshua was clothed with..." what?

5. "For behold the stone that I have laid before Joshua; upon one stone shall be seven..." what?

6. "...I have looked, and behold a candlestick all of gold, with a..." what?

7. "...What are these two olive trees upon the right side of the..." what?

8. What is an ephah?

9. "...behold, there came out two women, and the wind was in their wings; for they had wings like the wings of a..." what?

10. "...behold, there came four chariots out from between two mountains; and the mountains were mountains of..." what?

11. What was the color of the horses pulling the four chariots between the two mountains?

12. Fill in the blanks. "And the streets of the city shall be full of _____ and _____ playing in the streets thereof."

13. "And the LORD shall be king over all the..." what?

14. How many chapters are in Zechariah?

15. What book is after Zechariah?

MALACHI

QUESTIONS:

1. "If ye will not hear, and if you will not lay it to heart, to give glory unto my name, saith the LORD of hosts, I will even send a..." what?

2. "And this have ye done again, covering the altar of the LORD with..." what?

3. "And all nations shall call you..." what?

4. Was Elijah a prophet?

5. Is Malachi the last book of the Old Testament?

6. How many chapters are in Malachi?

Old Testament Answers

GENESIS

ANSWERS:

1. Heaven and earth.

2. The greater light was day and the other lesser light for night.

3. He made man and woman.

4. Ground.

5. A garden in Eden.

6. 1st, Pison; 2nd, Gihon; 3rd, Hiddekel; 4th, Euphrates

7. The tree of knowledge of good and evil.

8. Adam.

9. One of Adam's rib.

10. The serpent.

11. They put fig leaves on themselves.

12. "...clothed them."

13. Yes.

14. They had three sons.

15. The Bible mentions three—Cain, Abel, and Seth.

16. Cain killed Abel.

17. 930 years.

18. 912 years.

19. Noah.

20. Three.

21. Shem, Ham, and Zapheth.

22. An ark of gopher wood.

23. It was 450 feet long, 75 feet wide, and 45 feet high.

24. 40 days and 40 nights.

25. 8—Noah, his wife, their three sons, and their wives.

26. He was 600 years, 2 months, and 17 days.

27. 150 days.

28. "...and God made a wind to pass over the earth, and the waters asswaged";

29. A raven.

30. A dove.

31. Yes.

32. The dove brought back an olive leaf.

33. No— the dove did not come back.

34. "...and Noah removed the covering of the ark, and looked, and behold, the face of the ground was dry."

35. An altar.

36. He would never again destroy every living thing on earth.

37. "...Be fruitful, and multiply, and replenish the earth."

38. The blood.

39. "...by man shall his blood be shed..."

40. "And you, be ye fruitful, and multiply; bring forth abundantly in the earth, and multiply therein."

41. He would never again destroy the earth or man with a flood.

42. He puts a rainbow in the clouds.

43. Ham.

44. A vineyard.

45. By drinking wine.

46. 350 years.

47. A total of 950 years.

EXODUS

ANSWERS:

1. Pharaoh.

2. They made them work hard.

3. They were to kill him.

4. No.

5. He told the people they had to throw all baby boys in the river.

6. Jochebed.

7. Pharaoh's daughter.

8. Moses killed an Egyptian.

9. Zipporah.

10. "...put off thy shoes from off thy feet, for the place whereon thou standest is holy ground."

11. "...And Moses hid his face; for he was afraid to look upon God."

12. Back to Egypt.

13. His wife and his sons.

14. Pharaoh, the king of Egypt.

15. Aaron.

16. Moses was 80 years old and Aaron was 83 years old.

17. One score is 20 years.

18. Frog, lice, and flies.

19. Cattle, horses, donkeys, camels, oxen, and sheep.

20. Locust.

21. With an east wind.

22. Lamb.

23. 430 years.

24. To do their work and to serve them.

25. So the children of Israel could walk on dry ground through the sea. 14: 16-22

26. "...and the Lord overthrew the Egyptians in the midst of the sea. And the waters returned, and covered the chariots, and the horsemen, and all the host of Pharaoh that came into the sea after them; there remained not so much as one of them."

27. Red Sea.

28. An omer is a bundle of barley stocks. It is traditionally offered in Jewish Temples. They bake bread form the grain of those stocks.

29. So they would not have to work on the seventh day, which is the Sabbath.

30. Divinely supplied nourishment. Any food for the mind or spirit.

31. He told him to strike a rock.

32. Jethro.

33. They would die.

34. Exodus 20th chapter.

35. "...an altar of stone..."

36. Exodus chapter 21.

37. God said, "And he that smiteth his father, or his mother, shall be surely put to death."

38. Seventy.

39. There were twelve tribes.

40. Exodus 24th chapter, verse 12.

41. Exodus 24th chapter, verse 18.

42. Gold, silver, and brass.

43. Chapter 25, sixteen times.

44. Ten of linen or cloth, and one of goats hair.

45. Gold, brass, and silver.

46. It is the name of a tree. It is a thorn tree. The wood is hard and heavy.

47. Breastplate, ephod, robe, broidered coat, a mitre, and a girdle. An ephod is a linen apron. A Mitre is a cloth to be worn on the forehead.

48. Various units of weight. Gold weighing one shekel.

49. Eight times.

50. We should keep the sabbath day holy.

51. Leviticus, the third book of Moses.

LEVITICUS

ANSWERS:

1. The tabernacle.

2. Cattle, sheep, or goats.

3. They are meat, oil, flour, unleavened cakes, honey, salt, and ears of corn.

4. Without blemish. No marks on it.

5. They should not eat the fat or blood.

6. Bullock (a young bull), a young male goat, and a female lamb.

7. 18 times.

8. In Leviticus, chapter six and seven, it means different sins.

9. Girl babies, eighty days.

10. The test of leprosy.

11. The priest.

12. "And he shall break down the house, the stones of it, and the timber thereof, and all the mortar of the house; and he shall carry them forth out of the city into an unclean place."

13. Aaron's two sons.

14. In the wilderness.

15. The land of Canaan, especially with animals.

16. Idolatry, stealing, swearing, wages, adultry, brotherly love, weights and measures, sodomy, parents, incest, sorcery, gleanings, fitting, harlotry.

17. "...thou shalt neither sow thy field, nor prune thy vineyard. That which groweth of its own accord of thy harvest thou shalt not reap, neither gather the grapes of thy vine undressed: for it is a year of rest unto the land."

18. A Jubilee year is every 50th year. It followed the Sabbatic year.

19. There are 7 weeks between Passover and Pentecost. Tabernacles feast lasted 7 days. At Pentecost, 7 lambs were offered. Every 7th year is a Sabbatic year. Seven seals, seven trumpets, seven candlesticks, seven stars, seven angels, seven spirits, seven lamps, seven crowns, seven heads, seven kings, seven mountains, and many more.

20. The fourth Book of Moses—Numbers.

NUMBERS

ANSWERS:

1. To find out the number of men that were twenty years old and upward.
2. To find out how many men were able to go to war.
3. Dan, Asher, Nephtali, Benjamin, Merarites, Judah, Manasseh, Gershonites, Kohalhites, Ephriam, Zebulon, Gad, Simeon, and Reuben.
4. 46,500.
5. Levites.
6. 603,550.
7. Badgers skins. A badger is an animal that will weigh up to 25 lbs. It has a stiff fur, a small head, and short, heavy clawed legs.
8. A little over a bushel.
9. One male lamb, one female lamb, and one ram.
10. "...bless thee, and keep thee: The LORD make his face shine upon thee, and be gracious unto thee: The LORD lift up his countenance upon thee, and give thee peace."
11. Six covered wagons and twelve oxen.
12. Twenty-four. Oxen are the same as bullocks.
13. "...cleanse them."
14. Like fire.
15. It rested in the wilderness of Paran.
16. Judah led the march.
17. They were going from Sinai to Canaan.
18. Miriam.
19. Leprosy.
20. 12—the leaders of the tribes.
21. No, they turned back. Two did not.
22. Caleb and Joshua.
23. Korah. Chapter 16.
24. His failure to give God credit for the miracle of water. Chapter 20:10-12.
25. Miriam died at Kadesh, Aaron at Mt. Hor, and Moses in Mt. Nebo. Duet. 32:50

26. The second census.

27. The sacred year began in the spring. The civil year began in the fall.

28. Gold, silver, brass, iron, tin, and lead.

29. 123 years old.

30. It was 40 years from coming out of Egypt till he died.

31. Miriam was about 130 years old. Moses was 120 years old.

32. The fifth book of Moses—Deuteronomy.

DEUTERONOMY

ANSWERS:

1. Second law, or repetition of the law.

2. Abraham, Isaac, and Jacob.

3. The Ten Commandments.

4. Exodus, chapter 20.

5. He wrote them on two tablets of stone.

6. Moses.

7. We are to obey the Lord and keep his commandments, or this great fire will consume us.

8. "And thou shalt love the LORD they God with all thy heart, and with all thy soul, and with all thy might."

9. We should be continually teaching our children all of God's commandments whenever we possibly can. "...and shalt talk of them when thou sittest in thine house, and when thou walkest by the way, and when thou liest down, and when thou risest up."

10. "...for thou art a stiffnecked people."

11. When he opened the Red Sea and drowned Pharaoh and his army, feeding over 600,000 Israelites in the wilderness, and opening the earth and swallowing up Dathan and Abiram and their households.

12. The three great feasts were called the Feasts of Passover, Pentecost, and Tabernacles.

13. Bezer, Ramoth, and Golan.

14. Faint hearted, planted a new vineyard, built a new house, and newly married.

15. Women should not wear men's clothes, and men should not wear women's clothes.

16. Whole stones that were plastered.

17. Twelve.

18. The eagle was the emblem of the Roman army.

19. They ate them. Deuteronomy 28:58-57

20. They were to serve God, the way of life; or serve idols, which is certain death. Deuteronomy 29:17, 18, 26; 30:6, 15, 17, 18

21. He was 120 years old.

22. Joshua, the son of Nun.

23. 90th Psalm.

24. Moses died on Mt. Pisgah, in the land of Moab, at age 120.

25. The book of Joshua.

JOSHUA

ANSWERS:

1. Nun.

2. "Be strong and of a good courage:..."

3. Rahab.

4. They are in Gilgal and in the middle of the Jordan River.

5. The passover on the plains of Jericho.

6. About three miles, or half way between the Jordan and Jericho. Gilgal is Joshua's headquarters.

7. About seven acres.

8. When the priests blew their trumpets and all the people shouted very loudly at the same time, the walls fell down.

9. There were two walls. They were 15 feet apart. The outside wall was 6 feet thick, the inside wall was 12 feet thick, and they were about 30 feet high.

10. They burnt the city, the houses alongside the wall, and all their food supplies (mostly wheat, barley, dates, and lentils).

11. "...thirty thousand mighty men of valour..."

12. They set the city on fire.

13. They hanged him on a tree, and then they took his body down and piled stones on top of it.

14. The King of Jerusalem, King of Hebron, King of Jarmuth, King of Lachish, and King of Eglon.

15. The city of Gibeon called Joshua to come and save them from the Amorites. Joshua and his men went from Gilgal to Gibeon and fought the Amorites. During the battle, the sun and the moon stood still for one day. Joshua and his men defeated the Amorites.

16. Joshua hanged them on five trees.

17. Thirty-one are named. There could have been more.

18. "If ye forsake the LORD, and serve strange gods, then he will turn and do you hurt, and consume you, after that he hath done you good."

19. He was 110 years old.

20. In Mount Ephraim, on the north side of the hill of Gaash.

21. The Book of Judges.

JUDGES

ANSWERS:

1. Judah.

2. Simeon.

3. "...and they pursued after him, and caught him, and cut off his thumbs and his great toes."

4. "And they forsook the LORD God of their fathers, which brought them out of the land of Egypt, and followed other gods, of the gods of the people that were round about them, and bowed themselves unto them, and provoked the LORD to anger."

5. "...Nevertheless, the LORD raised up judges, which delivered them out of the hand of those that spoiled them."

6. While he was asleep, she took a nail of the tent and a hammer and drove the nail into his temples. Sisera died.

7. Jesus fasted 40 days and sojourned 40 days after the resurrection. Saul, David, and Solomon each reigned 40 years. During the flood, it rained 40 days. Moses fled at 40, was in Midian 40 years, and was in the mount 40 days. Israel wandered 40 years. The spies were in Canaan 40 days. Levi stayed in the mount 40 days and 40 nights.

8. Gideon.

9. Gideon.

10. Because Gideon feared his father's household and the men of the city.

11. Gideon's father was Joash.

12. 300 men.

13. One hundred and twenty thousand.

14. Gideon told the men of Israel, "I will not rule over you, neither shall my son rule over you: the LORD shall rule over you."

15. There were one thousand seven hundred shekels of gold. That would equal about seventeen thousand pounds of gold.

16. "And when he set the brands on fire, he let them go into the standing corn of the Philistines, and burnt up both the shocks, and also the standing corn, with the vineyards and olives."

17. He put the jawbone in his hand and killed a thousand men. Chapter 15

18. Twenty years.

19. Samson was very strong. After the Philistines put out his eyes, they stood him between two large pillars of the house that was full of men, women, and the lords of the Philistines. He gave a pull on both middle pillars and the house fell down and killed Samson and all the lords and people in it.

20. Samson.

21. The book of Ruth.

RUTH

ANSWERS:

1. King David.

2. Ten years.

3. Naomi—eight times.

4. Barley.

5. Naomi.

6. King David. It was the family of King David that our Saviour came from.

7. The field belongs to Boaz.

8. Obed. He is the Father of Jesse, the father of David.

9. First book of Samuel.

I SAMUEL

ANSWERS:

1. Ramah, about six miles north of Jerusalem.
2. His northern office was in Bethel. His western office was in Mizpah, three miles west of Namah.
3. Hannah.
4. She had four sons and two daughters.
5. Four times.
6. Eli. Eli's house and sons were wicked.
7. About 34,000.
8. When Eli heard his two sons Hophni and Phinehas were dead and the ark of God was taken, he fell backwards and broke his neck.
9. Eli was 98 years old.
10. A sucking lamb as a burnt offering.
11. He went to Bethel, Gilgal, and Mizpeh.
12. Gilgal.
13. Samuel called unto the Lord, and the Lord sent a severe thunder and rainstorm.
14. Saul did not keep the commandment.
15. In chapter 13, his successes went to his head. In chapter 14, his silly order for the army to abstain from food and his senseless death sentence for Jonathan showed the people what a fool they had for a king. In chapter 15, he had deliberate disobedience to God.
16. David.
17. A bear and a lion.
18. Five smooth stones.
19. He took Goliath's sword and cut off his head.
20. David took Goliath's head to Jerusalem and to Saul.
21. 9 feet tall.
22. Saul took a sword and fell upon it.
23. Second Book of Samuel.

II SAMUEL

ANSWERS:

1. Abner.

2. Abner hit Asahel under the fifth rib.

3. He wrote a letter to Joab.

4. Solomon.

5. Set it on fire.

6. He hanged himself.

7. The sword killed Twenty thousand men. The wood killed many more. (The battle was partly in a wooded area.)

8. He rode his mule under an oak tree and the branches caught him. While he was hanging there, Joab took three darts and thrust them through his ear.

9. Amasa.

10. Six fingers on each hand and six toes on each foot.

11. Four.

12. David.

13. Chapter 22:5

14. "...Shall seven years of famine come unto thee in thy land? Or wilt thou flee three months before thine enemies, while they pursue thee? Or that there be three days' pestilence in thy land?..."

15. "So the LORD sent a pestilence upon Israel..."

16. "...So David bought the threshingfloor and the oxen..."

17. The Kingdom, and the Psalms.

18. First book of the Kings.

I KINGS

ANSWERS:

1. Clothes.
2. The servants found a beautiful girl to try and warm the King.
3. Abishag.
4. Solomon.
5. King David.
6. Solomon.
7. "And keep the charge of the LORD thy God, to walk in his ways, to keep his statutes, and his commandments, and his judgments, and his testimonies..."
8. In the city of David.
9. Forty years. Seven years in Hebron and thirty-three years in Jerusalem.
10. Benaiah.
11. Egypt.
12. One thousand.
13. They are prostitutes.
14. Forty thousand.
15. Temple or church.
16. Cedar. They also used fir and olive trees.
17. Gold.
18. Seven years.
19. Solomon.
20. Red Sea.
21. Seven hundred wives.
22. Forty years.
23. In the city of David with his father.
24. His son, Rehoboam.
25. Twenty-two.
26. Seventeen years.
27. Twenty-four. One yoke is two animals.
28. Three years.
29. Jehoshaphat.
30. "And a certain man drew a bow at a venture, and smote the king of Israel between the joints of the harness..."
31. Twenty-two.
32. Second book of The Kings.

II KINGS

ANSWERS:

1. Elijah.

2. "And there came down fire from heaven, and consumed him and his fifty."

3. "...Elijah went up by a whirlwind into heaven."

4. Mantle.

5. "...Go up, thou bald head; go up, thou bald head."

6. "...and there came forth two she bears out of the wood, and tare forty and two children of them."

7. He was a leper.

8. "Then went he down, and dipped himself seven times in Jordan, according to the saying of the man of God: and his flesh came again like unto the flesh of a little child, and he was clean."

9. II Kings 5:27

10. Jezebel.

11. Seventy.

12. "And it came to pass, when the letter came to them, that they took the king's sons, and slew seventy persons, and put their heads in baskets, and sent him them to Jezreel. And there came a messenger, and told him, saying, They have brought the heads of the king's sons. And he said, Lay ye them in two heaps at the entering in of the gate until the morning."

13. Babylon.

14. The first book of The Chronicles.

I CHRONICLES

ANSWERS:

1. Begat.

2. "...So Saul took a sword, and fell on it."

3. "...looking out at a window saw king David dancing and playing: and she despised him in her heart."

4. "...idols: but the LORD made the heavens."

5. "...six on each hand, and six on each foot..." for a total of twenty-four.

6. A threshingfloor is where they put the entire stock of grain on a floor and beat on it to separate the grain from the stock and chaff.

7. David.

8. Shewbread is twelve loaves of consecrated unleavened bread formerly displayed in the Jewish temple. There was one for each tribe.

9. Twelve.

10. Second book of Chronicles.

II CHRONICLES

ANSWERS:

1. David.

2. Wisdom and knowledge.

3. Chariots and horsemen.

4. Cedar, fir, and algum.

5. In Jerusalem.

6. Gold.

7. Solomon.

8. Forty years.

9. His son Rehoboam.

10. "...and about the time of the sun was going down he died."

11. "...and he reigned twenty-five years in Jerusalem..."

12. In the city of David.

13. One hundred and thirty years old.

14. Jericho.

15. Ezra.

EZRA

ANSWERS:

1. Persia.

2. Babylon.

3. Chapter 2.

4. He was a priest.

5. Twenty-two.

6. The Book of Nehemiah.

NEHEMIAH

ANSWERS:

1. "...the gates thereof were consumed with fire."

2. Repaired.

3. "...and when he opened it, all the people stood up."

4. "...And all the people answered, Amen, with lifting up their hands: and they bowed their heads, and worshipped the LORD with their faces to the ground."

5. Israel.

6. Esther.

ESTHER

ANSWERS:

1. Red, blue, white, and black.

2. They were dead.

3. Yes.

4. Ester.

5. "...Then the king said, Hang him thereon."

6. "...and let Haman's ten sons be hanged upon the gallows."

7. "...and that he and his sons should be hanged on the gallows." 9:25

8. Mordecai the Jew, and Esther.

9. The book of Job.

10. Mordecai the Jew.

JOB

ANSWERS:

1. "And there were born unto him seven sons and three daughters."

2. "...and smote Job with sore boils from the sole of his foot unto his crown."

3. Sackcloth—that's like burlap.

4. One hundred and forty years.

5. The Book of Psalms.

PSALMS

ANSWERS:

1. "...handywork."

2. "...Lord our God."

3. "My God, my God, why hast thou forsaken me?..."

4. "The Lord is my shepherd; I shall not want."

5. God.

6. Blood.

7. One hundred and fifty.

8. 117 with 33 words.

9. Psalm 119 with 176 verses.

10. Proverbs.

PROVERBS

ANSWERS:

1. "...Egypt."

2. "...wisdom: and the knowledge of the holy is understanding."

3. "...mother."

4. "...rot."

5. "...lies."

6. "...depart from it."

7. "...fire that saith not, it is enough."

8. Ecclesiastes.

ECCLESIASTES

ANSWERS:

1. "...die..."

2. "...laugh; a time to mourn, and a time to dance";

3. "...embracing";

4. "...speak";

5. "...dust again."

6. "...birth."

7. "...forgotten."

8. "...fountain, or the wheel broken at the cistern."

9. Song of Solomon.

SONG OF SOLOMON

ANSWERS:

1. Solomon.

2. "...because the sun hath looked upon me:..." while he was working in his mother's vineyards.

3. Green.

4. Chariot.

5. Twins.

6. Eight.

7. Isaiah.

ISAIAH

ANSWERS:

1. "...the whole head is sick, and the whole heart is faint."

2. Amoz.

3. "...plowshares..."

4. Each seraphim had six wings.

5. "...Immanuel."

6. Honey.

7. "...chariots, and the horsemen shall set themselves in array at the gate."

8. "...broken in pieces;..."

9. LORD, LORD, LORD.

10. The language was Syrian.

11. Cedars and fir.

12. "...the earth;..."

13. Wine and milk.

14. A legendary serpent that is hatched by a reptile from a cock's egg and that has deadly glance. (*Webster's Dictionary*)

15. Chapter 66, verse 22.

16. Sixty-six.

17. Jeremiah.

JEREMIAH

ANSWERS:

1. Israel.

2. Trumpet.

3. "The children gather the wood."

4. Blue and purple.

5. Judas killed himself.

6. Nebuchadnezzar.

7. "...nations..."

8. Heaven and earth.

9. They cast him into the dungeon.

10. The Chaldeans.

11. By the swords, by the famine, and by the pestilence.

12. "Babylon is suddenly fallen and destroyed..."

13. "...threshingfloor..."

14. They broke down all of the walls of Jerusalem.

15. Fifty-two.

16. Lamentations.

LAMENTATIONS

ANSWERS:

1. "...bones..."

2. "...river day and night..."

3. "...wait for him, to the soul that seeketh him."

4. Five.

5. The book of Ezekiel.

EZEKIEL

ANSWERS:

1. "And every one had four faces, and every one had four wings."

2. "...idols; and turn away your faces from all your abominations."

3. Noah, Daniel, and Job.

4. "...die..." 18:20

5. Brass, tin, iron, lead, and silver.

6. It is the scum that forms on the surface of molten metal as it is melted.

7. Fir, cedar, and oak.

8. Forty years.

9. A cloud.

10. Sword.

11. The word gate is used over forty times and the word cubit is used over thirty five times.

12. Nine.

13. Sabbath, new moon. 46:1.

14. Daniel.

DANIEL

ANSWERS:

1. The city of Babylon.

2. Nebuchadnezzar, the king of Babylon.

3. In Jerusalem, about 603 years B.C.

4. "Nebuchadnezzar dreamed dreams, wherewith his spirit was troubled, and his sleep brake from him."

5. Daniel, Hananiah, Mishael, and Azariah.

6. "...Thy dream, and the visions of thy head upon thy bed..."

7. Babylonian, Persian, Greek, and Roman.

8. It was 114 inches in height and 128 inches across.

9. "And he commanded the most mighty men that were in his army to bind Shadrach, Meshach, and Abednego, and to cast them into the burning fiery furnace."

10. 586 before Christ.

11. "...a tree in the midst of the earth, and the height thereof was great." It made shade for all the animals, for all the birds, and fruit for all the people. "I saw in the visions of my head upon my bed, and behold, a watcher and an holy one came down from heaven; He cried aloud, and said thus, Hew down the tree, and cut off his branches, shake off his leaves, and scatter his fruit: let the beasts get away from under it, and the fowls from his branches: Nevertheless leave the stump of his roots in the earth, even with a band of iron and brass, in the tender grass of the field; and let it be wet with the dew of heaven, and let his portion be with the beasts in the grass of the earth. Let his heart be changed from man's, and let a beast's heart be given unto him: and let seven times pass over him."

12. Belshazzar, the same man is Daniel.

13. 70 years. He was over 90 years old when Darius conquered Babylon.

14. "...he kneeled upon his knees three times a day, and prayed and gave thanks before his God, as he did aforetime."

15. No.

16. Idol worshipping.

17. They ate them and broke all their bones.

18. Lion, Bear, Leopard, and a terrible beast.

19. Napoleon, Kaiser, and Hitler.

20. King Cyrus.

21. Daniel should return to fight with the prince of Persia.

22. Syria is called kings of the north. Kings of Egypt are called kings of the south.

23. The kings of the north.

24. Knowledge is increasing and travel is fast. For example, computers, books, newspapers, radios, television, trains, automobiles, ships, and airplanes.

25. "...Daniel: for the words are closed up and sealed till the time of the end."

26. Hosea.

HOSEA

ANSWERS:

1. "...Joash, king of Israel."

2. Gomer.

3. **Swearing** is the **2nd** commandment; **Lying** is the **8th** commandment; **Killing** is the **5th** commandment; **Stealing** is the **7th** commandment; **Adultery** is the **6th** commandment.

4. A dove.

5. Syria.

6. Fourteen.

7. Joel.

JOEL

ANSWERS:

1. 1) Palmerworm—a caterpillar that suddenly appears in great numbers devouring grass, and is destructive to fruit trees.

    2) Locust—a migratory grasshopper, stripping the areas of all vegetation.

    3) Cankerworm—any of various insect larva that inquire plants by feeding on buds and foliage.

    4) Caterpillar—a wormlike larva of a butterfly or moth.

2. Lion, lion. Lion.

3. Trumpet.

4. "...withdraw their shining."

5. Former, rain, former, latter.

6. "...blood..."

7. Wine.

8. Swords, spears.

9. "...Jehoshaphat: for there will I sit to judge all the heathen round about."

10. Wine, milk, and water.

11. Three.

12. Amons.

AMOS

ANSWERS:

1. Cedars and oaks.
2. "...good..."
3. A plumbline.
4. "...sword..."
5. "...darken the earth in the clear day":
6. "...hearing the words of the LORD":
7. "...melt."
8. Nine.
9. Obadiah.

OBADIAH

ANSWERS:

1. "...heathen..."
2. Grapes.
3. One.
4. Jonah.

JONAH

ANSWERS:

1. Wind, tempest.

2. "...he lay, and was fast asleep."

3. Hebrew.

4. A great fish swallowed him up.

5. "...And Jonah was in the belly of the fish three days and three nights."

6. "Then Jonah prayed unto the LORD his God out of the fish's belly."

7. "And the LORD spake unto the fish, and it vomited out Jonah upon the dry land."

8. Nineveh.

9. Sackcloth.

10. Four.

11. Micah.

MICAH

ANSWERS:

1. "...evil..."

2. Plowshares, pruninghooks.

3. One year old.

4. "...reap..."

5. "...mother, the daughter in law against her mother in law..."

6. Seven.

7. Nahum.

NAHUM

ANSWERS:

1. "...dry..."

2. "...and drieth up all the rivers;..."

3. "...red..."

4. "...torches, they shall run like the lightnings."

5. Ethiopia and Egypt.

6. Three.

7. Habakkuk.

HABUKKUK

ANSWERS:

1. "...Awake..."

2. "...Arise, it shall teach!..."

3. "...temple..."

4. "...afraid..."

5. Three.

6. Zephaniah.

ZEPHANIAH

ANSWERS:

1. "...sea..."
2. "...apparel."
3. "...inhabit them..."
4. "...darkness,"
5. "...dung."
6. Silver, gold, wrath, fire, dwell.
7. "...Gomorrah..."
8. Cedar. Cedar.
9. "...lions..."
10. Jealousy.
11. Ethiopia.
12. Jerusalem.
13. Three.
14. Haggai.

HAGGAI

ANSWERS:

1. Yes.
2. "...holes."
3. "...house; and I will take pleasure in it, and I will be glorified, saith the LORD."
4. Haggai.
5. "...dry land";
6. "...Haggai..."
7. Two.
8. Zechariah.

ZECHARIAH

ANSWERS:

1. "...evil ways, and from your evil doings..."

2. "...red horse..."

3. Myrtle trees.

4. "...filthy garments, and stood before the angel."

5. "...eyes..."

6. "...bowl upon the top thereof":

7. "...candlesticks..."

8. Hebrew unit of dry measure equal to 1/10 homer or a little over a bushel.

9. "...stork..."

10. "...brass."

11. "In the first chariot were red horses; and in the second chariot black horses; And in the third chariot white horses; and in the fourth chariot grisled and bay horses."

12. Boys, girls.

13. "...earth..."

14. Fourteen.

15. Malachi.

MALACHI

ANSWERS:

1. "...curse upon you, and I will curse your blessings: yea, I have cursed them already, because ye do not lay it to heart."

2. "...tears, with weeping, and with crying out, insomuch that he regardeth not the offering any more, or receiveth it with good will at your hand."

3. "...blessed..."

4. Yes.

5. Yes.

6. Four.

New Testament Questions

MATTHEW

QUESTIONS:

1. Who were Jesus' parents?
2. How many generations are between Abraham to David and David to Babylon, and Babylon to Christ? The number is the same on all three.
3. When Joseph found out Mary was pregnant, what did he want to do with her?
4. "And she shall bring forth a son, and thou shalt call his name JESUS: for he shall save his people from their..." what?
5. When Jesus was born, who gave Jesus his name?
6. Where was Jesus born?
7. Who was king when Jesus was born?
8. "When Herod the king had heard these things, he was..." what?
9. What country is Bethlehem in?
10. Fill in the blanks. "Then Herod, when he had privily called the _____ _____, enquired of them diligently what time the star appeared."
11. What led the wise men to where baby Jesus was?
12. When the wise men saw baby Jesus, what did they do?
13. The wise men presented baby Jesus with three gifts. What were they?
14. Did the wise men tell King Herod when they found baby Jesus?
15. Who warned the wise men not to return to King Herod or tell him where Jesus and Mary were?
16. Fill in the blank. "...the angel of the Lord appeareth to Joseph in a dream, saying, Arise, and take the young child and his mother, and flee into _____, and be thou there until I bring thee word: for Herod will seek the young child to destroy him." (It is the country Joseph and Mary went to with baby Jesus.)
17. Herod was very angry when the wise men did not come back and tell him where Jesus was. What order did he give out?
18. When Herod died, an angel told Joseph to take the child and his mother to what country?
19. In chapter 3, who was preaching in the wilderness of Judaea?
20. What foods did John the Baptist eat when he was in the wilderness?
21. "Then cometh Jesus from Galilee to Jordan unto John, to be..." what?
22. "And Jesus, when he was baptized, went up straightway out of the water: and, lo, the heavens were opened unto him, and he saw..." what?

23. "Then was Jesus led up of the spirit into the wilderness to be tempted of the..." who?

24. In chapter 4, how many days and nights was Jesus in the wilderness fasting?

25. After Jesus fasted, he was hungry. What did the tempter tell Jesus to do with the stones?

26. Jesus did not make bread out of the stones. "But he answered and said, It is written, Man shall not live by bread alone, but by every..." what?

27. "Jesus said unto him, It is written again, Thou shalt not tempt the..." who?

28. Finish the tenth verse in chapter four, "...Thou shalt worship the Lord thy God, and him only shalt..." what?

29. Fill in the blanks. "Now when Jesus had heard that John was cast into _____, he departed into _____";

30. Who were the two men Jesus saw casting their nets into the sea when he was walking by the Sea of Galilee?

31. What did Jesus say to Peter and Simon? It went like this, "Follow me, and I will make you..." what?

32. "Beware of false prophets, which come to you in sheep's clothing, but inwardly they are..." what?

33. Name the twelve disciples?

34. In chapter 10:29, what is the name of the bird?

35. In the parable of the sower, what did he sow?

36. What was Joseph's occupation?

37. In chapter 14, whom did Herod put in prison?

38. At Herod's birthday party Philip's wife danced for Herod. He liked her so much he said he would giver her anything she asked. What did she ask?

39. How many loaves and fishes did the disciples give Jesus to feed the multitude of people?

40. When the multitude of people got filled, how many baskets full of food were left?

41. In the evening that Jesus fed the multitude with five loaves and two fishes, how many people were there?

42. "And when the disciples saw him walking on the sea, they were troubled, saying, It is a..." what?

43. When Jesus was walking on the sea, what disciple got out of the ship and walked on the water to go to Jesus?

44. In chapter 16 Jesus asked his disciples, "Whom do men say that I the Son of man am?" Which disciple answered, "Thou art the Christ, the Son of the living God"?

45. When Jesus told his disciples, how had to go "...and suffer many things of the elders and chief priests and scribes, and be killed, and be raised again the third day. What was the town where he had to go?

46. In chapter 17, Peter said to Jesus, "...let us make here three tabernacles; one for thee, and one for..." what two other men?

47. In chapter 20 there was a man that hired laborers to work in his vineyard. How much did he pay them per day?

48. How many disciples did Jesus take up to Jerusalem?
49. When Jesus went to Jerusalem and took the twelve disciples, he said to them on the way, "Behold, we go up to Jerusalem: and the Son of man shall be betrayed unto the chief priests and unto the scribes, and they shall condemn him to death, And shall deliver him to the..." who?
50. "And as they departed from Jericho, a great multitude followed him. And, behold, two blind men sitting by the way side, when they heard that Jesus passed by, cried out saying, Have mercy on us, O Lord, thou son of David." What did they want Jesus to do for them?
51. In chapter 21, Jesus went to the temple. What did he do inside the temple?
52. What group of people say there is no resurrection?
53. "...If a man die, having no children, his brother shall marry his wife, and raise up seed unto his brother." How many brothers are there?
54. In chapter 22, God said, "I am the God of Abraham, and the God of Isaac, and the God of..." who?
55. There were ten virgins that went to meet the bridegroom. What did they take with them?
56. What time of the day or night did the bridegroom come?
57. Now when Jesus was in Bethany, in the house of Simon the leper, "There came unto him a woman having an alabaster box of..." what?
58. What did she do with the precious ointment?
59. "Then one of the twelve, called Judas Iscariot, went unto the chief priests, And said unto them, What will ye give me, and I will deliver him unto you?..." What was their reply?
60. Jesus sat down with the twelve and said, "Verily I say unto you, that one of you shall betray me." "And they were exceeding sorrowful, and began every one of them to say unto him, Lord is it I? And Jesus said, "The Son of man goeth as it is written of him: but woe unto that man be whom the Son of man is betrayed! It had been good for that man if he had..." what?
61. "And as they were eating, Jesus took bread, and blessed it, and brake it, and gave it to the disciples, and said,..." what?
62. "And he took the cup, and gave thanks, and gave it to them, saying,..." what?
63. Was this the last time Jesus drank from the fruit of the vine with His disciples?
64. After Jesus was risen from the dead, what town did He go to?
65. What was the sign Judas gave the multitude with swords that came to take Jesus away?
66. After Jesus was arrested by the crowd and taken away, what did the disciples do?

67. The crowd took Jesus to Caiaphas, the high priest's palace. It was at this palace that another disciple denied Him. Who said he did not know Jesus?

68. What disciple denied that he knew Jesus three times?

69. "Then began he to curse and to swear, saying, I know not the man. And immediately the..." what?

70. "When the morning was come, all the chief priests and elders of the people took counsel against Jesus to put him to death: And when they had bound him, they led him away, and delivered him to ..." who?

71. What did Judas do with the thirty pieces of silver he received for betraying Jesus?

72. How did Judas' life end?

73. "And the chief priests took the silver pieces, and said, It is not lawful for to put them into the treasury, because it is the price of blood." So, what did they buy with it?

74. What other name is potter's field called?

75. "And Jesus stood before the governor: and the governor asked him, saying, "Art thou the King of the Jews? And Jesus said unto him, ..." what?

76. Pilate, the governor, had a notable prisoner. He asked the people which one they wanted to go free - Jesus or the prisoner. What was the prisoner's name?

77. After Pilate released Barabbas, what did the multitude say to do with Jesus?

78. When Pilate saw that he could do nothing to convince the multitude to let Jesus go, he took water. What did he do with it?

79. The soldiers took Jesus into the governor's headquarters, "And they stripped him, and put on him a..." what?

80. What did the soldiers put on Jesus' head?

81. "And they spit upon him, and took the reed, and smote him on the head. And after that they had mocked him, they took the robe off form him, and put..." what?

82. After the soldiers put his own clothes back on him, they "led him away to..." what?

83. Who did the soldiers tell to help carry his cross?

84. Where did they take Jesus and the cross?

85. What did they give Jesus to drink before they crucified him?

86. After they crucified him, what did they do with his garments?

87. When Jesus was on the cross, they put a sign or accusation over his head. What did it say?

88. After Jesus was on the cross for six hours, what happened to the sky?

89. "And about the ninth hour Jesus cried with a loud voice, saying..." what?

90. One of Jesus' disciples went to Pilate "...and begged the body of Jesus. Then Pilate commanded the body to be delivered." Who was the disciple?

91. "And when Joseph had taken the body, he wrapped it in a clean linen cloth, And..." what?

92. How did the great stone get rolled away from Jesus' tomb?

93. What were the women's names that went to the tomb to find Jesus?

94. After Jesus arose from the dead, what town did he go to first?

95. What book follows Matthew?

MARK

QUESTIONS:

1. Did John baptize in the wilderness?
2. In what river did John baptize the people that were from Judaea and Jerusalem?
3. What was John clothed with?
4. After John baptized Jesus in the Jordan, what did the heavens and the Spirit do?
5. What did the voice form heaven say?
6. "And immediately the spirit driveth him into..." where?
7. How long was Jesus in the wilderness?
8. When Jesus walked by the sea of Galilee, what two men did he see casting nets into the sea?
9. As Simon and Andrew were coming in from fishing, "And Jesus said unto them, Come ye after me, and I will make you to become..." what?
10. "And when he had gone a little farther thence, he saw ..." what two other men mending their nets?
11. Simon did not have a wife. True or False?
12. "And he began again to teach by the sea side: and there was gathered unto him a great multitude, so that he entered into a ..." what?
13. "And he said unto them, Is a candle brought to be put under a bushel, or under a..." what?
14. "If any man have ears to hear..." what three words?
15. "The sower soweth the word." True or False?
16. "...And the unclean spirits went out, and entered into the swine: and the herd ran violently down a steep place into the sea..." How many were there?
17. There was a woman that hemorrhaged for twelve years and could not get well. For she said, "If I may touch but his clothes, I shall be whole." She did touch his clothes, and Jesus said, "Who touched by clothes?" The woman told Jesus it was her. "And he said unto her..." what?
18. How old was the little girl that Jesus took by the hand and said, "...Damsel, I say unto thee, arise."
19. How did John the Baptist die?
20. In what place did the executioner behead John the Baptist?
21. Jesus asked the disciples, "How many loaves have ye? Go and see." How many did they have?
22. Fill in the blank. "And they did all eat, and were filled. And they took up _____ baskets full of the fragments, and of the fishes."

23. About how many men did Jesus feed?

24. After the people were done eating, what did Jesus tell his disciples to get into?

25. "And when he had sent them away, he departed into a..." where?

26. What happened to the blind man when Jesus put his hand on his eyes?

27. "And he saith unto them, But whom say ye that I am? And Peter answereth and saith unto him..." what?

28. But when he had turned about and looked on his disciples, he rebuked Peter, saying, ..." what?

29. What three disciples did Jesus take up into the mountain?

30. When Peter, James, and John went up in the high mountain, what happened to Jesus?

31. After the transfiguration, what color did his cloths become?

32. What will happen to the person that offends a little child that believes in Jesus?

33. Jesus said, "...My house shall be called of all nations the house of..." what?

34. "The baptism of John, was it from heaven, or of men? Answer me." The men did not know. What was Jesus' answer?

35. There was a woman who had an alabaster box. What was in the box?

36. What did the woman do with the precious ointment?

37. Jesus said, "...I will smite the shepherd, and the sheep shall be..." what?

38. In what town will Jesus go after he is risen?

39. "But he held his peace, and answered nothing. Again the high priest asked him, and said unto him, Art thou the Christ, the Son of the Blessed?" What was Jesus' answer?

40. What disciple denied Jesus three times after the cock crowed twice?

41. The elders, scribes, and the whole council took Jesus to what man?

42. "And Pilate asked him, Art thou the King of the Jews? And he answering said unto him..." what?

43. Who was the prisoner that Pilate released to the people?

44. When the soldiers led Jesus away, what color of clothes did they put on him?

45. What did the people put on Jesus' head?

46. When they led Jesus out to crucify him they took off the purple clothes. What did they put back on him?

47. Where did they take Jesus to be crucified?

48. Who were the two men they compel to bear the cross?

49. After they crucified Jesus, what did they do with his clothes?

50. "And the superscription of his accusation was written over,..." What did the inscription read?

51. There were other men being crucified. One on Jesus' right and the other on Jesus' left. What kind of criminals were they?

52. What happened when the sixth hour came?

53. When Jesus was still on the cross, "And at the ninth hour Jesus cried with a loud voice, saying,..." what?

54. When Jesus was still on the cross, what did a man put on a sponge to give Jesus to drink?

55. What did the centurion say when he was facing Jesus on the Cross and Jesus took his last breath?

56. Who were the two women looking on from a distance as Jesus was still on the cross?

57. What was the day after the preparation day?

58. Who did Pilate give Jesus' body to?

59. Who took Jesus down from the cross?

60. Who were the three women that bought sweet spices to anoint Jesus?

61. "Now when Jesus was risen early the first day of the week, he appeared first to..." who?

62. When Jesus was taken up into heaven, which side of God did he sit on?

63. How many chapters are in the book of Mark?

64. What chapter is after Mark?

LUKE

QUESTIONS:

1. Who was the king of Judaea?

2. Did Elisabeth have any children? Yes or No.

3. What was Zacharias' wife's name?

4. Zacharias and Elisabeth had a son. What was his name?

5. "And it came to pass in those days, that there went out a decree from Caesar Augustus, that all the world should be..." what?

6. What town is called the city of David?

7. In what city was baby Jesus born?

8. In what country were the shepherds in when they saw the light when Jesus was born?

9. How many shepherds went to Bethlehem to see baby Jesus?

10. Who or what brought the message to the shepherds in the form of a star or light?

11. When the shepherds got to Bethlehem, what three people did they find in the stable?

12. Mary said the baby she was to have would be called Jesus. Who decided on his name?

13. After Jesus was circumcised on the eighth day, what town did they go to?

14. Who did Joseph and Mary take baby Jesus to when they got to Jerusalem?

15. "(As it is written in the law of the Lord, Every male that openeth the womb shall be called holy to the Lord;) And to offer a sacrifice according to that which is said in the law of the Lord, A pair of ..." what birds are to be used as sacrifices?

16. Who was the man waiting in the temple to see Jesus? This is the same man that, "Then took he him up in his arms, and blessed God, and said, Lord, now lettest thou thy servant depart in peace, according to thy word: For mine eyes have seen thy salvation, Which thou hast prepared before the face of all people; A light to lighten the Gentiles, and the glory of thy people Israel."

17. Who and what was Anna?

18. When Joseph, Mary, and Jesus left Jerusalem, what country and city did they go to?

19. Jesus and his parents usually went to Jerusalem to the passover every year. How old was Jesus the year his parents discovered he was not with them?

20. When Jesus' parents went back to Jerusalem to look for him, where did they find him?

21. John said, "Whose fan is in his hand, and he will thoroughly purge his floor, and will gather the wheat into his garner; but the chaff he will..." what?

22. Who had John put in prison?

23. When Jesus returned from Jordan, where did the spirit lead him?

24. How many days was Jesus tempted in the wilderness by the devil?

25. Who told Jesus, "If thou be the Son of God, command this stone that it be made into bread."?

26. "And Jesus answered him, saying, It is written, That man shall not live by bread alone, but by..." what?

27. Satan said to Jesus that if Jesus would worship him he would give Jesus all this power and glory. "And Jesus answered and said unto him..." what?

28. There were two ships standing by the lake Gennesaret. When the people pressed against Jesus, he got in one of the ships. What did he do in the ship?

29. Who owned the ship that Jesus taught from?

30. "Now when he had left speaking, he said unto Simon..." what?

31. What two men were Simon's partners in the ship when they filled the ship with fish?

32. Fill in the blanks. "And it came to pass, when he was in a certain city, behold a man full of _____: who seeing Jesus fell on his face, and besought him, saying, Lord, if thou wilt, thou canst make _____ _____."

33. What was Levi's job or profession?

34. When Jesus and his disciples went through the cornfield plucking the ears of corn, what day was it?

35. After Jesus chose his twelve disciples, "...he lifted up his eyes on his disciples, and said, Blessed be ye poor: for yours is the..." what?

36. What would they get when he said, "Blessed are ye that hunger now: for ye shall..." what?

37. Jesus went to a city called Nain. "Now when he came nigh to the gate of the city, behold, there was a dead man carried out, ..." What did he say to the young man?

38. What prophet did Jesus say was the greatest prophet?

39. What did they put in an alabaster box?

40. After the woman washed Jesus' feet, what did she do with the ointment?

41. What happened to the seed that fell upon a rock? "And some fell upon a rock; and as soon as it was sprung up,..." what happened?

42. "Now the parable is this: The seed is the..." what three words?

43. When Jesus was in a ship with his disciples, Jesus said to them, "Let us go over unto the other side of the lake." While they were sailing, what did Jesus do?

44. While Jesus was asleep in the ship, what did the weather do?

45. When Jesus was in the boat with his disciples, he fell asleep. A great storm came and the disciples awoke him. What were the four words Jesus said to them?

46. When Jesus and His disciples arrived on the other side of the lake, a man that was full of devils came running to Jesus. Jesus asked, "What is thy name?" What did he say his name was?

47. This man Legion was full of devils. Where did the devils go when they left his body?

48. After the devils or demons entered the swine, where did the swine go?

49. "...Jairus, and he was a ruler of the synagogue: and he fell down at Jesus' feet, and besought him that he would come into his house." His daughter was dying. How old was the daughter?

50. What three apostles did Jesus take up into the mountain to pray?

51. As Jesus was praying, his face changed. What color did his clothes turn to?

52. Jesus turned to the disciples and said something private to them. What did He say?

53. Martha had a sister. What was her name?

54. As Jesus was "praying in a certain place," what did one of his disciples ask Jesus to do for them?

55. Jesus said, "He that is not with me is..." what?

56. How many sparrows are mentioned in chapter 12 verse 6?

57. What happened to the rich man when he pulled down his barns and built new and bigger barns to store his many goods?

58. Fill in the blank. "For where your treasure is, there will your_____ be also."

59. When Jesus said to all people, "I tell you, Nay: but, except ye repent, ye shall all likewise..." what?

60. A man had a fig tree that did not bear fruit for three years. What did he tell the gardener to do with it?

61. Did Jesus heal anyone on the sabbath? Yes or No?

62. Jesus healed a woman on the sabbath. What was her father's name?

63. Finish this verse. "Strive to enter in at the strait gate..." then what?

64. When you prepare a big dinner or feast as the Bible calls it, who should you invite?

65. What did the beggar Lazarus have all over his body?

66. When Lazarus was full of sores, who came and licked his sores?

67. When the beggar Lazarus died, the angels came. Where did the angels carry him?

68. The rich man died and was buried. In hell, who did he see afar off?
69. "And as he entered into a certain village, there met him ten men that were...which stood afar off. What disease did they have?
70. When Jesus saw these ten lepers, where did he tell them to go and show themselves?
71. When the ten lepers were made well, how many turned back to Jesus and thanked him?
72. "But the same day that Lot went out of Sodom it..." what did the weather do?
73. "But Jesus called them unto him, and said, Suffer little children to come unto me, and forbid them not: for..." what?
74. As Jesus "...come nigh unto Jericho, a certain blind man sat by the way side begging:" "And he cried, saying, Jesus, thou son of David, have mercy on me." What did this man ask Jesus to do for him?
75. What was Zacchaeus's job or profession?
76. Zacchaeus was very poor. True or False?
77. What did Zacchaeus do so he could see Jesus?
78. When Jesus "...was coming nigh to Bethphage and Bethany, at the mount called the mount of Olives, he sent two of his disciples," to go into town and get him—what?
79. When the disciples brought the colt to Jesus, what did they do with the colt?
80. Jesus went into the temple and said, "...My house is the house of prayer, but ye have made it a..." what?
81. "The baptism of John, was it from heaven, or of men?"
82. "There were therefore seven brethren: and the first took a wife, and died without children. And the second took her to wife, and he died childless. And the third took her; and in like manner the seven also: and they left no children, and died." How many children did he have?
83. After the seven brothers died, what happened to the woman?
84. God said, "For he is not a God of the dead, but of the..." what?
85. How many tribes were there in Israel?
86. What disciple approached Jesus to kiss him?
87. What disciple denied Jesus three times?
88. "And the whole multitude of them arose, and led him unto..." who?
89. Were Pilate and Herod friends?
90. What was the name of the place they crucified Jesus?
91. When Jesus and the two criminals hung on the cross, what did Jesus say?
92. What did they do with Jesus' clothing?

93. While Jesus was on the cross, the soldiers mocked him. What did the soldiers offer him?

94. "And the soldiers said, "...If thou be the king of the Jews,..." Jesus should what?

95. One of the criminals said to Jesus, "...Lord, remember me when thou comest into thy kingdom." What was Jesus' answer?

96. What hour was it when darkness was over all the earth?

97. On the cross Jesus cried with a loud voice. What did he say?

98. "Now when the centurion saw what was done, he glorified God saying,..." what?

99. Who took Jesus' body off of the cross?

100. What did Joseph do with Jesus' body?

101. "And the women also, which came with him from Galilee, followed after, and beheld the sepulchre, and how his body was laid. And they returned, and prepared..." what?

102. The eleven people and those that were with them gathered together "Saying, The Lord is risen indeed, and hath appeared to..." who?

103. "And as they thus spake, Jesus himself stood in the midst of them, and saith unto them,..." what?

104. Jesus showed the people his hands and feet. They still did not believe him. Then, he asked them for something to eat. What did they give him?

105. Where was Jesus carried up to when he lifted up his hands and blessed them?

106. How many chapters are there in Luke?

107. What book follows Luke?

JOHN

QUESTIONS:

1. "There was a man sent from God, whose name was..." what?
2. "For the law was given by Moses, but grace and truth came by..." who?
3. "...when the Jews sent priests and Levites from Jerusalem..." what question did they ask John?
4. After John was asked a number of times who he was, who did he say he was?
5. What river was John baptized in?
6. When Jesus went to Jerusalem and to the temple, what three live things were they selling?
7. Why did men love darkness rather than light?
8. What will we have when verse thirty-six chapter three says, "He that believeth on the Son hath..." what?
9. When Jesus was sitting on Jacob's well, a Samaritan woman came to get water. What did Jesus ask her to do for Him?
10. When Jesus met the woman at the well, what kind of water did he ask her to give him?
11. How many husbands did the woman at the well have?
12. God is a spirit. Is that true or false?
13. In what place did Jesus change the water into wine?
14. Jesus said, "...The hour is coming, in the which all that are in the graves shall hear his voice, And shall come forth; they that have done good, unto the resurrection of life; and they that have done evil, unto the resurrection of damnation." What two places will each one go?
15. "And Jesus went up into a mountain, and there he sat with..." who?
16. When Jesus came down from the mountain a great multitude of people were to be feed. Who had the two small fish and the five barley loaves for Jesus to feed the five thousand people?
17. How many baskets of food fragments were left?
18. After Jesus fed the five thousand, where did he go alone?
19. When Jesus was still up in the mountain, the disciples went to the sea and got in a ship to go to Capernaum. They were about four miles out when the sea got rough and they were afraid. Then, they saw Jesus walking on the sea. What did Jesus say to them?
20. "After these things Jesus walked in Galilee: for he would not walk in Jewry, because..." why?
21. The law is the Ten Commandments. Who gave Moses the commandments?

22. "In the last day, that great day of the feast, Jesus stood and cried saying, If any man thirst, let him come unto me, and..." what?
23. What two groups of people took the adulterer's woman out to be stoned in front of Jesus?
24. The stone killed the adulterous woman. True or False?
25. Jesus said, "And ye shall know the truth, and the truth shall make you..." what?
26. Who was Jesus talking about when he said, "...He was a murderer form the beginning, and abode not in the truth, because there is no truth in him. When he speaketh a lie, he speaketh of his own: for he is a liar, and the father of it."?
27. "...he spat on the ground, and made clay of spittle, and he..." what?
28. On what day did Jesus make clay and caused the blind man to see?
29. When Jesus said, "I am the good shepherd: the good shepherd giveth his life for the..." what?
30. When Jesus said, "I and my Father are one. Then the Jews took up stones again to stone him." Who were they going to stone?
31. Why were the Jews going to stone Jesus?
32. What town did Lazarus get sick in?
33. Mary had a sister. What was her name?
34. Martha and Mary had a brother. What was his name?
35. What are the two words in chapter eleven verse 35?
36. When Lazarus died and was laid in the tomb, Jesus came to the tomb and cried with a loud voice. What did he cry out?
37. How many days was Lazarus dead when Jesus got to the tomb?
38. Where was the Jews passover held?
39. Who were the chief priests and the Pharisees looking for?
40. Six days before the passover, Jesus went to Bethany. Martha made Jesus' supper. Who "...was one of them that sat at the table with him."?
41. What house did Jesus go to in Bethany when Martha made him supper?
42. What did Mary do with a pound of ointment?
43. After Mary put ointment on Jesus' feet, one of his disciples said the ointment should have been sold and the money given to the poor. Which disciple said that?
44. What disciple betrayed Jesus?

45. What else did Jesus say when he said, "For the poor always ye have with you; but..." what?

46. Jesus said, "He that loveth his life shall lose it; and he that hateth his life in this world shall keep it unto..." what?

47. Jesus said, "Father, glorify thy name." What did the voice from heaven say?

48. What did Jesus come to do when he said, "...I came not to judge the world, but to..." what?

49. After supper Jesus took a towel and poured water into a bason. Who's feet did he wash?

50. Did Jesus wash Simon Peter's feet?

51. Jesus said, "In my Father's house are many mansions:." What did he say he would do for us?

52. What disciple cut off a servant's right ear with a sword?

53. "And Simon Peter stood and warmed himself. They said therefore unto him, Art not thou also one of his disciples? He denied it, and said, I am not." Then, the man that Peter cut off his ear asked, "Did not I see thee in the garden with him? Peter then denied again: and immediately..." what happened?

54. What man asked the people, "What accusation bring ye against this man?"

55. "...The Jews therefore said unto him, It is not lawful for a Jew to put any man...." what?

56. "And the soldiers platted a crown of thorns, and put it on his head, and they put on him a..." what color of robe?

57. What reason did the Jews give that Jesus should die?

58. What was the name of the place where Jesus carried the cross?

59. "And Pilate wrote a title, and put it on the cross..." What was the title or inscription?

60. While Jesus was on the cross his mother was standing by. What did he say to her?

61. "...Jesus knowing that all things were now accomplished, that the scripture might be fulfilled, saith,..." what?

62. What did they put on a sponge and put to Jesus' mouth?

63. After Jesus received the vinegar, what did he say?

64. What did the soldiers do to the legs of the two criminals who were hanging beside Jesus, but did not do to Jesus' legs?

65. Who died first, the criminals or Jesus?

66. Joseph went to Pilate. What did he ask for?

67. Who was the first person to come to the sepulchre and find the stone taken away from the tomb?

68. Who did Mary Magdalene run to when she saw the stone had been taken away from the sepulchre?

69. Mary stayed weeping after the people left the sepulchre. As she looked in the tomb, what did she see besides the napkin and linen clothes?

70. "Then the same day at evening, being the first day of the week, when the doors were shut where the disciples were assembled for fear of the Jews, came Jesus and stood in the midst, and saith unto them,..." what?

71. Who did Jesus tell, "Reach hither thy finger, and behold my hands; and reach hither thy hand, and thrust it into my side: and be not faithless, but believing."?

72. After Thomas touched Jesus' side, what did Thomas say to Jesus?

73. In the book of John, how many times does it say the words, "Verily, verily, I say unto you" or "Verily, verily, I say unto thee"?

74. How many chapters are in the book of John?

75. What book is after John?

ACTS

QUESTIONS:

1. "...Judas, which was a guide to those that took Jesus. For he was numbered with us, and had obtained part of this ministry. Now this man purchased a field with the reward of iniquity..." What happened to him when he fell headlong in the field?
2. What did they name the field where Judas lost his bowels?
3. "And suddenly there came a sound from heaven as of a rushing mighty wind, and it filled all the house where they were sitting." What kind of tongues appeared?
4. "And it shall come to pass in the last days, saith God, I will pour out of my Spirit upon all flesh: and your sons and your daughters shall prophesy, and your young men shall see visions, and your old men shall..." what?
5. "And I will shew wonders in heaven above, and signs in the earth beneath;...." What are the signs below?
6. In the last days what will the sun be turned into?
7. In the last days what will the moon be turned into?
8. "...The LORD said unto my Lord, Sit thou on my right hand. Until I make thy foes thy..." what?
9. The people said to Peter and the apostles, "Men and brethren, what shall we do?" What two things did Peter tell them to do?
10. Where did Peter and John go together to pray?
11. Who did the partriarchs sell to Egypt?
12. There came a famine in Egypt and Canaan. What kind of grain did Jacob find in Egypt and "...he sent out our fathers first."?
13. What country did Jacob go to and die?
14. "Then said the Lord to him, Put off thy shoes from thy feet: for the place where thou standest is..." what kind of ground"?
15. What kind of a calf did they make for an idol?
16. "...at Joppa a certain disciple named Tabitha, which by interpretation is called is called..." what?
17. What did Dorcas make for widows?
18. Dorcas got sick and died. Who came and knelt down and prayed? He said, "Tabitha, arise..."?
19. What did Peter do when he went up on the housetop?
20. The Lord said, "John indeed baptized with water; but ye shall be baptized with the..." what?
21. King Herod had James the brother of John killed. What kind of weapon was used?

22. Herod had Peter put in prison. How did Peter get out of prison?
23. "...Herod, arrayed in royal apparel, sat upon his throne, and made an oration unto them." What did God do to him?
24. How did Herod die after the angel struck him down?
25. How many nations did God destroy in the land of Chanaan?
26. What happened to Paul and Silas when they were taken to the marketplace and to the magistrates?
27. What nationality was Paul and Silas?
28. Paul and Silas were put in prison. While in prison, their feet were put in stocks. How did they get out of prison?
29. What did Paul and Silas tell the jailer when he asked them, "What must I do to be saved?"
30. As John passed by the altar, what was the inscription on the altar?
31. "And the times of this ignorance God winked at; but now commandeth all men every where to ..." what?
32. God, "hath appointed a day, in the which he will judge the world in righteousness by that man whom he hath ordained;..." Who is that man?
33. "Then spake the LORD to Paul in the night by a vision, Be not afraid, but ..." what?
34. What was Jesus' answer when he said, "I have shewed you all things, how that so labouring ye ought to support the weak, and to remember the words of the Lord Jesus, how he said,..."?
35. How many daughters did Philip the evangelist have?
36. How many chains did the chief captain demand Paul be bound with?
37. "For the Sadducees say that there is no resurrection, neither angel, nor spirit: but the Pharisees confess both." What two things do the Pharisees confess to?
38. Paul was a leader of what sect of religion?
39. The Bible says, "And have hope toward God, which they themselves also allow, that there shall be a resurrection of the dead, both of the ..." what?
40. Chapter 26 verse 15 reads, "And I said, Who art thou, Lord? And he said..." what?
41. "And as he thus spake for himself, Festus said with a loud voice,..." what?
42. What country did they take Paul and some prisoners to?
43. When Paul was a prisoner, he and the other prisoners were delivered to a man in Italy. Who was the man?
44. The ship that Paul and the prisoners were on wrecked. What happened to them?
45. What was the name of the island that Paul and the prisoners swam to?
46. "...Paul had gathered a bundle of sticks, and laid them on the fire,...." What came out of the fire and was on his hand?

47. The Bible says a "viper" or "venomous beast" hung on Paul's hand. How did he get this off and what did he do with it?

48. At the very end of the book of Acts, Paul was preaching and teaching about the Lord Jesus Christ. What place did he do this teaching and preaching?

49. How many chapters are in the book of Acts?

50. What book follows the book of Acts?

ROMANS

QUESTIONS:

1. Paul said, "For I am not ashamed of the gospel of Christ: for it is the power of God unto salvation to every one that believeth; to the Jew first, and also to the..." who?

2. What shall the just live by?

3. "Professing themselves to be wise, they became..." what?

4. "And even as they did not like to retain God in their knowledge, God gave them over to a..." what kind of mind?

5. Verse 29 says, "Being filled with all unrighteousness..." What are some of the bad things people say and do?

6. In chapter three, what popular verse says, "As it is written, There is none righteous, no, not one:"?

7. In chapter three it says,"Their throat is an open sepulchre;...." What do they do with their tongues?

8. What is their mouth full of?

9. "Their feet are swift to shed..." what?

10. What two nationalities are mentioned several times in chapter three?

11. Fill in the blank. "..._____; who is the father of us all,"

12. "Therefore being justified by faith, we have peace with God through our..." what?

13. "For when we were yet without strength, in due time Christ died for..." who?

14. "But God commendeth his love toward us, in that, while we were yet sinners, Christ..." did what?

15. "For the wages of sin is..." what?

16. What free gift does God give us?

17. When people live in the flesh, they are not pleasing - who?

18. If we live fleshly, we will surely—what?

19. "...ye have received the Spirit of adoption, whereby we cry..." what?

20. "And we know that all things work together for good to them that love..." who?

21. "...If God be for us, who can..." what?

22. "Who shall separate us from the love of Christ? Shall..." what seven things?

23. What are the ten things that will not "...be able to separate us from the love of God, which is in Christ Jesus our Lord"?

24. "It was said unto her, The elder shall serve the..." who?

25. Fill in the blank. Rebecca said, "...Jacob have I loved, but _____have I hated."

26. "Hath not the potter power over the ..." what?

27. "For Christ is the end of the law for righteousness to every one that..." what?

28. "For the gifts and calling of God are without..." what?

29. "Therefore if thine enemy hunger,..." we should do what?

30. "...if he thirst,..." we should do what?

31. "Be not overcome of evil, but overcome evil with..." what?

32. "Whosoever therefore resisteth the power, resisteth the ordinance of God: and they that resist shall receive to themselves..." what?

33. God says, "Owe no man anything, but to love one another: for he that loveth another..." what

34. What are the five commandments mentioned in chapter 13?

35. God said, "...if there be any other commandment, it is briefly comprehended in this saying, namely, Thou shalt..." what?

36. The Lord said, "For whether we live, we live unto the Lord; and weather we die, we die unto the Lord: weather we live therefore, or die, we are the..." who's?

37. "For to this end Christ both died, and rose, and received, that he might be Lord both of the..." what?

38. We should not judge our brother, "...for we shall all stand before the judgement seat of..." who?

39. God said, "For the kingdom of God is not meat and drink; but..." what three things?

40. "We then that are strong ought to bear the infirmities of the..." who?

41. Paul said, "But now having no more place in these parts,..." he went on a journey into what country?

42. Finish verse 33 of chapter 15, "Now the God..."

43. "Salute one another with an holy..." what?

44. How many chapters are in the book of Romans?

45. What book is after Romans?

I CORINTHIANS

QUESTIONS:

1. "Paul, called to be an apostle of ..." who?
2. ""Unto the church of God which is at..." where?
3. "Grace be unto you, and peace, from God our Father, and from the ..." who?
4. "For the preaching of the cross is to them that perish foolishness; but unto us which are saved it is the..." what?
5. "I have fed you with milk, and not with..." what?
6. "Know ye not that ye are the temple of God, and that the Spirit of God..." what?
7. "If any man defile the temple of God, him shall God..." what?
8. What does God say the temple is?
9. "I write not these things to shame you, but as my beloved sons I..." what?
10. "For the kingdom of God is not in word, but in..." what?
11. What kind of people will not inherit the kingdom of God?
12. "For ye are bought with a price: therefore glorify God in your..." what?
13. "Nevertheless, to avoid fornication, let every man have..." what?
14. "...and let every woman have..." what?
15. The bible says that they all drank from the spiritual rock. Who is the spiritual rock?
16. "...to the intent we should not lust after..." what?
17. "But I say, that the things which the Gentiles sacrifice, they sacrifice to..." who?
18. "For a man indeed ought not to cover his head, forasmuch as he is the image and glory of God: but the woman is the glory of the..." who?
19. Who was the woman created for?
20. What does chapter 11:14 say about a man with long hair?
21. "But if a woman have long hair, it is a..." what?
22. "But the manifestation of the Spirit is given to every man to profit withal." What are these that are mentioned in chapter 12 that are given by the spirit?
23. "And now abideth faith, hope, charity, these three; but the greatest of these is..." what?
24. "All flesh is not the same flesh:..." Name the four kinds of flesh mentioned in 15:39.
25. There are three glories in the sky. What are they?
26. There are two kinds of bodies. What are they?
27. "All the brethren greet you. Greet ye one another with an..."
28. The last verse of I Corinthians says, "My love be with you all in..." who?
29. How many chapters are in I Corinthians?
30. What is the book after I Corinthians?

II CORINTHIANS

QUESTIONS:

1. "Grace be to you and peace from God our Father, and..." what?

2. "...we should not trust in ourselves, but in..." who?

3. "For we walk by faith, not by..." what?

4. "Be ye not unequally yoked together with unbelievers: for what fellowship hath righteousness with unrighteousness? and what communion hath light with darkness?" In this verse what does yoked mean?

5. "Every man according as he purposeth in his heart, so let him give; not grudgingly, or of necessity:..." what?

6. "For his letters, say they, are..." what?

7. Paul had many perils. Name them.

8. In 11:27 there are eight things that Paul endured. What are they?

9. "Greet one another with an holy..." what?

10. "All the saints..." what?

11. How many chapters are in II Corinthians?

12. What book follows II Corinthians?

GALATIANS

QUESTIONS:

1. Was Paul one of the apostles?

2. "...if any man preach any other gospel unto you than that ye have received, let him be..." what?

3. "... no man is justified by the law in the sight of God, it is evident: for, The just shall live by..." what?

4. Fill in the blanks. "Wherefore _____ _____ was our schoolmaster to bring us unto Christ, that we might be justified by faith."

5. "For all the law is fulfilled in one word, even in this; Thou shalt love thy..." what?

6. Is witchcraft a sin?

7. Verse 21 of chapter 5 says "Envyings, murders, drunkenness, revellings, and such like: of the which I tell you before, as I have also told you in time past, that they which do such things shall not inherit..." what?

8. What is the fruit of the Spirit?

9. "If we live in the Spirit, let us also..." what?

10. "For if a man think himself to be something, when he is nothing, he..." what?

11. "For he that soweth to his flesh shall of the flesh reap..." what?

12. How many chapters are in Galatians?

13. What book follows Galatians?

EPHESIANS

QUESTIONS:

1. "And hath put all things under his..." what?

2. "...and gave him to be the head over all things to the..." what?

3. "For by grace are ye saved through..." what?

4. Who is the chief corner stone?

5. Who created all things?

6. "For this cause I bow my knees unto the..." who?

7. "Be ye therefore followers of God as dear..." what?

8. "And take the helmet of salvation, and the sword of the Spirit, which is the..." what?

9. "Grace be with all them that love our..." who?

10. How many books are in Ephesians?

11. What is the next book after Ephesians?

PHILIPPIANS

QUESTIONS:

1. "For me to live is Christ, and to die is..." what?
2. "Look not every man on his own things, but every man also on the things of ..." who?
3. Fill in the blanks. "That at the name of Jesus every _____ should bow, of things in _____, and things in _____, and things under the _____";
4. What should every tongue confess?
5. Fill in the blanks. "Beware of ____, beware of ____ ____, beware of ____."
6. Who should we rejoice in?
7. "Let your moderation be known unto..." who?
8. "Finally, brethren, whatsoever things are...if there be any virtue, and if there be any praise, think on these things." Name these things.
9. "I can do all things through..." who?
10. What is the last verse in the book of Philippians?
11. How many chapters are in the book of Philippians?
12. What is the next book after the book of Philippians?

COLOSSIANS

QUESTIONS:

1. "Paul, an apostle of ..." who?

2. Finish the verse. "Who hath delivered us from the power of darkness,..."

3. "Who is the image of the invisible God,...?"

4. God is the head of what body?

5. God said, "For though I be absent in the flesh, yet I am with you in the..." what?

6. What should we do after we receive Christ Jesus into our lives?

7. "Set your affection on things above, not on things on the..." what?

8. "When Christ, who is our life, shall appear, then shall ye ..." what?

9. "Mortify therefore your members which are upon the earth;..." What five things are they?

10. "But now ye also put off all these;..." What are the five things?

11. Fill in the blank. "And above all these things put on _____, which is the bond of perfectness."

12. "And whatsoever ye do in word or deed, do all in the name of the..." who?

13. Fill in the blank. "Wives, _____ yourselves unto your own husbands, as it is fit in the Lord." 3:18

14. Fill in the blank. "Husbands, _____ your wives, and be not bitter against them." 3:19

15. What does verse 3:20 say about children and their parent? "Children..."

16. "The salutation by the hand of me Paul. Remember my bonds...." What are the last five words?

17. How many chapters are in the book of Colossians?

18. What is the book after Colossians?

I THESSALONIANS

QUESTIONS:

1. The people were worshipping idols. Who did they finally turn to worship?

2. "For now we live, if we stand fast in the..." who?

3. Who directs our way?

4. "For God hath not called us unto uncleanness, but unto..." what?

5. "For the Lord himself shall descend from heaven with a shout, with the voice of the archangel, and with the trump of God: and the dead in Christ shall..." what?

6. When the Lord returns, He will come like a...what?

7. "For God hath not appointed us to wrath, but to ...what?

8. 5:15 says, "See that none render evil for evil unto any man; but ever follow that which is good, both among yourselves, and to all men." What are verses 5:16-22 that tell us what God wants us to do so we can live good and without evil?

9. How many chapters are in I Thessalonians?

10. What is the book after I Thessalonians?

II THESSALONIANS

QUESTIONS:

1. "For the mystery of iniquity doth already..." finish the verse.

2. Fill in the blank. "Therefore, brethren, stand fast, and hold the _____ which ye have been taught, whether by word, or our epistle."

3. "Comfort your hearts, and stablish you in every good..." what two things?

4. "...for all men have not..." what

5. "For even when we were with you, this we commanded you, that if any would not work, neither should he..." what?

6. "Now the Lord of peace himself give you peace always by all means..." What is the last sentence of this verse?

7. How many chapters are in II Thessalonians?

8. What book is after II Thessalonians?

I TIMOTHY

QUESTIONS:

1. "Now the end of the commandment is charity out of a pure heart, and of a good..." what? Finish the verse.

2. "Knowing this, that the law is not made for a righteous man, but for the..." who?

3. Who did Christ Jesus come into the world to save?

4. "For there is one God, and one mediator between God and men,..." Who is that?

5. "I will therefore that men pray every where, lifting up..." what?

6. Women should dress modestly. What does 2:9 say women should not do?

7. Who was first formed, Adam or Eve?

8. What should we be holding the mystery of faith in?

9. "And without controversy great is the mystery of godliness:..." What are the six things?

10. What are the things you must insist on and teach?

11. "Lay hands suddenly on no man, neither be partaker of other men's sins: keep thyself..." what?

12. 5:23 says, "Drink no longer water, but use a little wine for thy..." what?

13. "For we brought nothing into this world, and it is certain we can...what?

14. "For the love of money is the root of all..." what?

15. "Be thou, O man of God, flee these things; and follow after..." what?

16. How many chapters are in I Timothy?

17. What is the book after I Timothy?

II TIMOTHY

QUESTIONS:

1. "Paul, an apostle of Jesus Christ by the will of..." who?

2. "For God hath not given us the spirit of fear;..." But He has given us the spirit of what three things?

3. "It is a faithful saying: For if we be..." what?

4. In 2:20 fill in the blanks. "But in a great house there are not only vessels of _____ and of _____, but also of _____ and of _____; and some to honour, and some to dishonour."

5. Fill in the blank. "This know also, that in the last days _____ times shall come."

6. In the last days what are some characteristics that men will have?

7. Finish verse 4:7. "I have fought a good fight, I have finished my course,..."

8. What are the last five words of the book of II Timothy?

9. How many chapters are in II Timothy?

10. What is the book after II Timothy?

TITUS

QUESTIONS:

1. "But a lover of hospitality, a lover of..." what?

2. "Exhort servants to be obedient unto their own..." who?

3. 3:3 talks about some of the wrongful ways one can behave and think. What are they?

4. Titus ordained the first bishop of what church?

5. How many chapters are in Titus?

6. What book follows Titus?

PHILEMON

QUESTIONS:

1. "Hearing of thy love and faith, which thou hast toward the..." who?

2. "If he hath wronged thee, or oweth thee ought, put that..." where?

3. How many chapters are in Philemon?

4. What is the book after Philemon?

HEBREWS

QUESTIONS:

1. "And of the angels he saith, Who maketh his angels spirits, and his ministers a flame of...what?

2. "Thou hast loved righteousness, and hated..." what?

3. "And, Thou, Lord, in the beginning hast laid the foundation of ..." what?

4. "For every house is builded by some man; but he that built all things is..." who?

5. "...To day; lest any of you be hardened through the deceitfulness of ..." what?

6. "For we are made partakers of..." who?

7. Fill in the blank. "...God did rest the _____ day from all his works."

8. If you listen to God's voice, your heart will not—what?

9. "For the word of God is quick, and powerful, and sharper than any ..." what?

10. "And after the second vail, the tabernacle which is called the..." what?

11. In 10:4 what two animals are mentioned?

12. In 11:2 what did the elders have?

13. Who was Abraham's son?

14. What was Abraham going to do to Isaac?

15. When Jacob was dying, who did he bless?

16. "By faith Joseph, when he died, made mention of the departing of the children of..." who?

17. Who's daughter found baby Moses hiding in the basket?

18. When the Red sea opened up, what group of people drowned?

19. Fill in the blank. "By faith the walls of _____ fell down, after they were compassed about seven days."

20. In 12:8 it says, "But if ye be without chastisement, whereof all are partakers, then are ye..."what?

21. Fill in the blank. "Lest there be any fornication, or porfane person, as ____, who for one morsel of meat sold his birthright."

22. "For our God is a consuming..." what?

23. Fill in the blanks. "Marriage is honourable in all, and the bed undefiled: but _____ and _____ God will judge."

24. "Salute all them that have the rule over you, and all the saints. They of _____ salute you."

25. How many chapters are in the book of Hebrews?

26. What is the book after Hebrews?

JAMES

QUESTIONS:

1. Who was James a servant of?

2. "Knowing this, that the trying of your faith..." what?

3. Finish verse 1:10 "But the rich, in that he is made low:..."

4. Fill in the blanks. "For if there come unto your assembly a man with a gold ring, in _____ apparel, and there come in also a poor man in ____ raiment";

5. "Behold, we put bits in the..." where?

6. Why do we put bits in horses' mouths?

7. It is very hard for man to control his tongue. What does God say about the evil tongue?

8. "...whosoever therefore will be a friend of the world is the enemy of..." who?

9. Fill in the blanks. "Submit yourselves therefore to ____. Resist the _____, and he will flee from you."

10. "Humble yourselves in the sight of the Lord, and he shall..." what?

11. Finish the verse. "Whereas ye know not what shall be on the morrow. For what is your life? It is even a..."

12. Fill in the blanks. "Your riches are _____, and your garments are _____."

13. "Your gold and silver is cankered; and the rust of them shall..." what?

14. Fill in the blanks. "Be ye also _____; stablish your _____: for the coming of the _____ draweth nigh."

15. Who is the man who prayed for it not to rain, and it didn't rain for three years and six months?

16. What happened when Elias prayed for rain?

17. "Let him know, that he which converteth the sinner from the error of his way shall..."what?

18. How many chapters are in the book of James?

19. What book is after James?

I PETER

QUESTIONS:

1. Was Peter an apostle of Jesus Christ?

2. 1:7 says that your faith is more precious than—what?

3. "Forasmuch as ye know that ye were not redeemed with corruptible things, as..." what two metals?

4. "But with the precious blood of Christ, as of a lamb without..." what?

5. "For all flesh is as..." what?

6. "...and all the glory of man as..." what?

7. "But the word of the Lord endureth..." how long?

8. "For the eyes of the Lord are over the..." who?

9. "...the face of the Lord is against them that do..." what?

10. How many people were saved when God flooded the earth in the times of Noah?

11. "Who is gone into heaven, and is on the..." what?

12. Fill in the blanks. "And above all things have fervent _____ among yourselves: for charity shall cover the _____ of ____."

13. "And when the chief Shepherd shall appear, ye shall receive a..."what?

14. Fill in the blank. "...for God resisteth the _____, and giveth grace to the _____."

15. Who should we cast all our cares to?

16. We should be vigilant and alert, because someone is waiting to devour us. Who is this one waiting to destroy us?

17. How many chapters are in the book of I Peter?

18. What is the book after I Peter?

II PETER

QUESTIONS:

1. God did not spare the angels when they sinned. Where did God cast them?

2. "For if God spared not the angels that sinned, but cast them down to hell, and delivered them into chains of darkness, to be reserved unto..." what?

3. 2:5 says Noah was "...a preacher of..." what?

4. What happened to the cities of Sodom and Gomorrha?

5. To the Lord, one day is like how many years?

6. Fill in the blank. "But the day of the Lord will come like a _____ in the night;..."

7. When the Lord comes, what will the heavens do?

8. What will happen to everything on earth?

9. How many chapters are in the book of II Peter?

10. What book follows II Peter?

I JOHN

QUESTIONS:

1. "If we say that we have no sin, we deceive..." who?

2. "And the world passeth away, and the lust thereof: but he that doeth the will of God..." what?

3. Cain was very wicked. What did he do?

4. "My little children, let us not love in word, neither in tongue; but in ..." what?

5. "He that loveth not knoweth not God; for God is ..." what?

6. Has any man ever seen God?

7. Why should we love God?

8. "If a man say, I love God, and hateth his brother, he is a..." what?

9. "For there are three that bear record in heaven,..." What are the three?

10. "And there are three that bear witness in earth,..." What are the three?

11. "All unrighteousness is..." what?

12. The last verse in the book of I John says, "Little children, keep yourselves from..." what?

13. How many chapters are in I John?

14. What book is after I John?

II JOHN

QUESTIONS:

1. Fill in the blanks. "For many deceivers are entered into the world, who confess not that Jesus Christ is come in the flesh. This is a _____ and an _____."

2. "Look to yourselves, that we lose not those things which we have wrought, but that we receive a..." what?

3. "...He that abideth in the doctrine of Christ, he hath both the..." what?

4. How many chapters are in the book of II John?

5. What is the book after II John?

III JOHN

QUESTIONS:

1. ""Beloved, follow not that which is evil, but that which is..." what?

2. Fill in the blanks. "...He that doeth _____ is of God: but he that doeth _____ hath not seen God."

3. How many chapters are in III John?

4. What book follows III John?

JUDE

QUESTIONS:

1. Who was Jude a servant of?

2. Who was Jude's brother?

3. "...Adam, prohesied of these, saying, Behold, the Lord cometh with..." How many saints?

4. How many chapters are in the book of Jude?

5. What book is after Jude?

REVELATION

QUESTIONS:

1. How many churches in Asia did John go to?
2. What does Alpha and Omega mean?
3. "...What thou seest, write in a book, and send it unto the..." what?
4. Fill in the blank. "And I turned to see the voice that spake with me. And being turned, I saw _____ golden candlesticks";
5. What was the color of the man's hair that was in the midst of the candlesticks?
6. What were his feet like?
7. What did his voice sound like?
8. What came out of his mouth?
9. "And when I saw him, I fell at his feet as dead. And he laid his right hand upon me, saying unto me,..." what?
10. Who said, "I am he that liveth, and was dead; and, behold, I am alive for evermore, Amen; and have the keys of hell and of death,"
11. What kind of sword is mentioned in 2:12?
12. Fill in the blanks. "Repent; or else I will _____ _____ _____ _____..."
13. Fill in the blanks. "He that hath an ear, _____ _____ _____ what the Spirit saith unto the churches; To him that overcometh will I give to eat of the _____ _____, and will give him a _____ _____, and in the stone a new name written, which no man knoweth saving he that receiveth it."
14. What does Jezebel call herself?
15. Jesus gave her an opportunity to repent of her fornication. Did she repent?
16. What did Jesus say he would do to her children?
17. What is mentioned in 3:7 that is the same name as a big town in eastern Pennsylvania?
18. "I know thy works: behold, I have set before thee an open door, and no man can..." what?
19. Fill in the blank. "...I will write upon him the name of the city of my God, which is new _____, which cometh down out of heaven from my God: and I will write upon him my new name."
20. "I know thy works, that thou art neither..." what?
21. "Behold, I stand at the door, and knock: if any man hear my voice, and open the door, I will..." what?
22. "And round about the throne were four and twenty seats: and upon the seats I saw..." what?
23. What was coming out of the throne?
24. What was before the throne?

25. There are four beasts around the throne. What animals are they like?

26. "And the four beasts had each of them six wings about him; and they were full of eyes within: and they rest not day and night, saying,..." what?

27. How many horns did the slain lamb have?

28. In chapter six, what color was the horse?

29. Another horse appeared after the second seal was open. What color was it?

30. When the third seal opened, what color of horse appeared?

31. What color was the horse after the fourth seal was opened?

32. "And I looked, and behold a pale horse: and his name that sat on him was..." what?

33. When the fifth seal was opened, what was under the altar?

34. What happened when the sixth seal opened?

35. "And cried with a loud voice, saying, Salvation to our God which sitteth upon the..." what?

36. Fill in the blanks. "For the Lamb which is in the midst of the throne shall _____ them, and shall _____ them unto living fountains of waters: and God shall wipe away all tears from their eyes."

37. "And when he had opened the seventh seal, there was..." what?

38. What kind of altar was before the throne?

39. "The first angel sounded, and there followed..." what?

40. "And the second angel sounded, and as it were a great mountain burning with fire was cast into..." where?

41. Fill in the blanks. "And the name of the star is called _____: and the third part of the waters became _____; and many men died of the waters, because they were made bitter."

42. When the fifth angel blew his trumpet, what fell from the sky?

43. What were the shapes of the locusts?

44. In 11:13 there was an earthquake. How many people were killed?

45. Fill in the blanks. "And there appeared a great wonder in heaven; a woman clothed with the _____, and the _____ under her feet, and upon her head a crown of _____ _____."

46. "And there appeared another wonder in heaven; and behold a great red dragon, having..." what?

47. Fill in the blanks. "He that leadeth into captivity shall _____ _____ _____: he that killeth with the sword must be _____ _____ _____ _____. Here is the patience and the faith of the saints."

48. Finish this verse. "Here is the patience of the saints: here are they that..."

49. "And I saw another sign in heaven, great and marvellous, seven angels having the..." what?

50. How were the seven angels dressed when they came out of the temple?

51. "And he gathered them together into a place called in the Hebrew tongue..." what?

52. "And there fell upon men a great hail out of heaven, every stone about the weight of a talent: and men..." what?

53. Fill in the blanks. "And there are _____ kings: _____ are fallen, and ____ is, and the other is not yet come; and when he cometh, he must continue a short space."

54. "And after these things I heard a great voice of much people in heaven, saying,..." what?

55. When heaven opened, who sat on the white horse?

56. "And he was clothed with a vesture dipped in blood: and his name is called..." what?

57. "And he hath on his vesture and on his thigh a name written,..." What is that name?

58. In 20:1, who had the key to the bottomless pit?

59. The angel with the key to the bottomless pit also had a chain. With that chain the angel bound up the dragon and Devil? How many years are they bound?

60. In 20:4, what will happen to those who take a stand for Jesus and for the word of God?

61. What will the reward be to the people who do not take the mark of the beast?

62. When the thousand-year reign ends, what will happen to Satan?

63. What will Satan do to "...the nations which are in the four quarters of the earth,..."?

64. "And the devil that deceived them was cast into the..." what?

65. If your name is not found in the book of life, when you die, where will you go?

66. What was the name of the holy city that John saw?

67. Fill in the blanks. "And he said unto me, It is done. I am _____ and _____, the _____ and the ____. I will give unto him that is athirst of the fountain of the water of life freely."

68. "And had a wall great and high, and had..." how many gates?

69. How many tribes are of the children of Israel?

70. Finish this verse. "Behold, I come quickly:..."

71. In 22:14, what is one's reward who does his commandments?

72. "For I testify unto every man that heareth the words of the prophecy of this book, If any man shall add unto these things, God shall..." what?

73. "And if any man shall take away from the words of the book of this prophecy, God shall..." what?

74. "He which testifieth these things saith,..." what?

75. What is the last verse of the Bible?

76. How many chapters are in the book of Revelation?

New Testament Answers

MATTHEW

ANSWERS:

1. Joseph and Mary.
2. Fourteen.
3. Put her away.
4. "...sins."
5. Joseph.
6. Bethlehem.
7. Herod.
8. "...troubled, and all Jerusalem with him."
9. Judaea.
10. Wise men.
11. The star they saw in the east went before them.
12. "...they saw the young child with Mary his mother, and fell down and worshipped him."
13. Gold, Frankincense, and myrrh.
14. No.
15. God warned them in a dream.
16. Egypt.
17. To kill all of the children in Bethlehem and along the coasts, two years old and under.
18. Israel.
19. John the Baptist.
20. Locusts and wild honey.
21. "...baptized of him."
22. "...the Spirit of God descending like a dove, and lightening upon him:".
23. "...devil."
24. Forty days and forty nights.
25. "...If thou be the Son of God, command that these stones be made bread."
26. "...word that proceedeth out of the mouth of God."
27. "...Lord thy God."
28. "...thou serve."

29. Prison, Galilee.

30. Simon called Peter and Andrew his brother.

31. "...fishers of men."

32. "...ravening wolves."

33. Simon, Peter, Andrew, James son of Zebedee, Bartholomew, Thomas, Matthew, John, James son of Alphaeus, Thaddaeus, Philip, and Judas Iscariot.

34. Sparrows.

35. Seeds.

36. Carpenter.

37. John the Baptist.

38. "...Give me here John Baptist's head in a charger."

39. Five loaves and two fishes.

40. Twelve baskets full.

41. "And they that had eaten were about five thousand men, beside women and children."

42. "...spirit; and they cried out for fear."

43. Peter.

44. Simon Peter.

45. Jerusalem.

46. "...Moses, and one for Elias."

47. One penny a day.

48. Twelve.

49. "...Gentiles to mock, and to scourge, and to crucify him: and the third day he shall rise again."

50. They were blind and, "They say unto him, Lord, that our eyes may be opened."

51. "And Jesus went into the temple of God, and cast out all them that sold and bought in the temple, and overthrew the tables of the moneychangers, and the seats of them that sold doves, And said unto them, It is written, My house shall be called the house of prayer; but ye have made it a den of thieves."

52. Sadducees. 22:23

53. "Now there were with us seven brethren:..."

54. "...Jacob..."

55. Lamps.

56. Midnight. 25:6

57. "...precious ointment..." 26:7

58. "...and poured it on his head, as he sat at meat."

59. "...And they covenanted with him for thirty pieces of silver."

60. "...not been born."

61. "...Take, eat; this is my body."

62. "...Drink ye all of it; For this is my blood of the new testament, which is shed fro many for the remission of sins."

63. Yes—"But I say unto you, I will not drink henceforth of this fruit of the vine, until that day when I drink it new with you in my Father's kingdom."

64. Galilee.

65. "...Whomsoever I shall kiss, that same is he: hold him fast."

66. "...Then all the disciples forsook him, and fled."

67. "...and a damsel came unto him, saying, Thou also wast with Jesus of Galilee."

68. Peter. 27:70-74

69. "...cock crew."

70. "...Pontius Pilate the governor."

71. He tried to give the money back to the chief priests and elders. They would not take it. So, "And he cast down the pieces of silver in the temple, and departed, and went and hanged himself."

72. He hung himself.

73. "And they took counsel, and bought with them the potter's field, to bury strangers in."

74. "Wherefore that field was called, The field of blood, unto this day."

75. "...Thou sayest."

76. Barabbas.

77. "...They all say unto him, Let him be crucified."

78. "...he took water, and washed his hands before the multitude, saying, I am innocent of the blood of this just person: see ye to it."

79. "...scarlet robe."

80. Crown of thorns.

81. "...his own raiment on him..."

82. "...crucify him."

83. Simon.

84. A place called Golgotha.

85. "They gave him vinegar to drink mingled with gall: and when he had tasted thereof, he would not drink." Gall is a bile obtained from an animal or something bitter to drink.

86. They cast lots or gambled for them.

87. "And set up over his head his accusation written, THIS IS JESUS THE KING OF THE JEWS."

88. "Now from the sixth hour there was darkness over all the land unto the ninth hour."

89. "...Eli, Eli, lama sabachthani? That is to say, My God, my God, why hast thou forsaken me?"

90. Joseph.

91. "...laid it in his own new tomb, which he had hewn out in the rock: and he rolled a great stone to the door of the sepulchre, and departed."

92. "And, behold, there was a great earthquake: for the angel of the Lord descended from heaven, and came and rolled back the stone from the door, and sat upon it."

93. "...Mary Magdalene and the other Mary to see the sepulchre."

94. Galilee.

95. Mark.

MARK

ANSWERS:

1. Yes.
2. Jordan.
3. "And John was clothed with camel's hair, and with a girdle of a skin..."
4. "And straightway coming up out of the water, he saw the heavens opened, and the Spirit like a dove descending upon him":
5. "Thou art my beloved Son, in whom I am well pleased."
6. "...the wilderness."
7. Forty days.
8. Simon and his brother Andrew.
9. "...fishers of men."
10. James and his brother John.
11. False. Simon did have a wife.
12. "...ship..."
13. "...bed? And not to be set on a candlestick?"
14. "...let him hear."
15. True.
16. "...(they were about two thousand;)..."
17. "...Daughter, thy faith hath made thee whole; go in peace, and be whole of thy plague."
18. Twelve.
19. "And immediately the king sent an executioner, and commanded his head to be brought: and he went and beheaded him in the prison."
20. In prison.
21. They had five loaves and two fishes.
22. Twelve.
23. About five thousand men.
24. Ship.
25. "...mountain to pray."

26. "After that he put his hands again upon his eyes, and made him look up: and he was restored, and saw every man clearly."

27. "...Thou art the Christ."

28. "...Get thee behind me Satan: for thou savourest not the things that be of God, but the things that be of men."

29. Peter, James, and John.

30. "...and he was transfigured before them."

31. White as snow.

32. "...it is better for him that a millstone were hanged about his neck, and he were cast into the sea."

33. "...prayer..."

34. "...Neither do I tell you by what authority I do these things."

35. Very precious ointment.

36. She poured it on Jesus' head.

37. "...scattered."

38. Galilee.

39. "And Jesus said, I am: and ye shall see the Son of man sitting on the right hand of power, and coming in the clouds of heaven."

40. Peter.

41. Pilate the King.

42. "...Thou sayest it."

43. Barabbas.

44. Purple.

45. A crown of thorns.

46. His own clothes.

47. Golgotha.

48. Simon and Rufus.

49. "And when they had crucified him, they parted his garments, casting lots upon them, what every man should take."

50. "...THE KING OF THE JEWS."

51. They were thieves.

52. "...there was darkness over the whole land until the ninth hour."

53. "Eloi, Eloi, lama sabachthani? Which is, being interpreted, My God, my God, why hast thou forsaken me?"

54. Vinegar.

55. "...Truly this man was the Son of God."

56. Mary Magdalene and Mary the mother of James.

57. The sabbath.

58. Joseph.

59. Joseph.

60. "...Mary Magdalene, and Mary the mother of James, and Salome, had brought sweet spices, that they might come and anoint him."

61. "...Mary Magdalene, out of whom he had cast seven devils."

62. "...and sat on the right hand of God."

63. Sixteen.

64. Luke.

LUKE

ANSWERS:

1. Herod.

2. No.

3. Elisabeth.

4. John.

5. "...taxed."

6. Bethlehem.

7. Bethlehem.

8. Judaea.

9. The Bible does not say how many there were?

10. Angels.

11. The shepherds found Mary, Joseph, and the baby Jesus.

12. An angel named him.

13. Jerusalem.

14. The Lord.

15. "...turtledoves, or two young pigeons."

16. Simeon.

17. A prophetess.

18. To the country of Galilee and the city of Nazareth.

19. Twelve years old.

20. In the temple.

21. "...burn with fire unquenchable."

22. Herod.

23. "...into the wilderness."

24. Forty days.

25. The devil.

26. "...every word of God."

27. "...Get thee behind me, Satan: for it is written, Thou shalt worship the Lord thy God, and him only shalt thou serve."

28. He taught the people.

29. Simon.

30. "...Launch out into the deep, and let down your nets for a draught."

31. James and John, the sons of Zebedee.

32. Leprosy, me, clean.

33. Tax collector.

34. Sabbath or Sunday.

35. "...kingdom of God."

36. "...be filled..."

37. "...Young man, I say unto thee, Arise."

38. John the Baptist.

39. Ointment.

40. She anointed His feet.

41. "...it withered away, because it lacked moisture."

42. "...word of God."

43. Jesus fell asleep.

44. "...and there came down a storm of wind on the lake; and they were filled with water, and were in jeopardy."

45. "Where is your faith?"

46. Legion.

47. They entered a heard of swine.

48. The herd ran violently into a lake where they drowned.

49. Twelve years of age.

50. Peter, John, and James.

51. "...white and glistering."

52. "...Blessed are the eyes which see the things that ye see:"

53. Mary.

54. "...Lord, teach us to pray, as John also taught his disciples."

55. "...is against me."

56. Five sparrows.

57. "But God said unto him, Thou fool, this night thy soul shall be required of thee:..."

58. Heart.

59. "...perish."

60. Cut it down.

61. Yes.

62. Abraham.

63. "...for many, I say unto you, will seek to enter in, and shall not be able."

64. "But when thou makest a feast, call the poor, the maimed, the lame, the blind":

65. He was, "full of scores".

66. The dogs.

67. "...into Abraham's bosom:..."

68. Abraham.

69. Leprosy.

70. Unto the priests.

71. Only one, a Samaritan.

72. "...it rained fire and brimstone from heaven, and destroyed them all."

73. "...such is the kingdom of God."

74. "...Lord, that I may receive my sight."

75. He was a chief tax collector.

76. False. He was very rich.

77. He climbed up into a sycomore tree.

78. A colt.

79. "And they brought him to Jesus: and they cast their garments upon the colt, and they set Jesus thereon."

80. "...den of thieves."

81. From heaven.

82. All seven died childless.

83. "Last of all the woman died also."

84. Living.

85. Twelve.

86. Judas.

87. Peter.

88. Pilate.

89. Yes.

90. Calvary.

91. "...forgive them; for they know not what they do..."

92. "...and they parted his raiment," (clothes) "and cast lots."

93. Vinegar.

94. "...save thyself."

95. "And Jesus said unto him, Verily I say unto thee, Today shalt thou be with me in paradise."

96. "And it was about the sixth hour, and there was a darkness over all the earth until the ninth hour."

97. "...Father, into thy hands I commend my spirit:..."

98. "...Certainly this was a righteous man."

99. Joseph.

100. "And he took it down, and wrapped it in linen, and laid it in a sepulchre that was hewn in stone, wherein never man before was laid."

101. "...spices and ointments;..."

102. "...Simon."

103. "...Peace be unto you."

104. "And they gave him a piece of a broiled fish, and of an honeycomb."

105. "...he was parted from them, and carried up into heaven."

106. Twenty-four.

107. John.

JOHN

ANSWERS:

1. "...John."

2. "...Jesus Christ."

3. "...Who art thou?"

4. "He said, I am the voice of one crying in the wilderness..."

5. Jordan.

6. Oxen, sheep, and doves.

7. "...because their deeds were evil."

8. "...everlasting life:..."

9. "...Give me to drink."

10. Living water.

11. She had five husbands.

12. True. "God is a Spirit: and they that worship him must worship him in spirit and in truth."

13. Cana in Galilee.

14. Heaven or hell.

15. "...his disciples."

16. A young boy.

17. Twelve baskets.

18. He went up into a mountain.

19. "It is I; be not afraid."

20. "...the Jews sought to kill him."

21. Jesus.

22. "...drink."

23. The scribes and Pharisees.

24. False. They dropped their stones and left.

25. Free.

26. Devil.

27. "...anointed the eyes of the blind man with the clay,"

28. On the sabbath.

29. The sheep.

30. Jesus.

31. ...for blasphemy; and because that thou being a man, makest thyself God."

32. Bethany.

33. Martha.

34. Lazarus.

35. "Jesus wept."

36. "Lazarus, come forth."

37. Four days.

38. Jerusalem.

39. Jesus.

40. Lazarus was one of them that sat at the table with him.

41. Lazarus.

42. She anointed the feet of Jesus, and wiped his feet with her hair.

43. Judas Iscariot.

44. Judas Iscariot.

45. "...me ye have not always."

46. "...life eternal."

47. "I have glorified it, and will glorify it again."

48. "...save the world."

49. The disciples' feet.

50. Yes.

51. "...I go to prepare a place for you."

52. Simon Peter.

53. "...the cock crew."

54. Pilate.

55. "...to death."

56. "...purple robe."

57. "...because he made himself the Son of God."

58. "The place of a skull, which is called in the Hebrew Golgotha."

59. "...JESUS OF NAZARETH THE KING OF THE JEWS."

60. "Woman, behold thy son!"

61. "I thirst."

62. Vinegar.

63. "It is finished":

64. The soldiers broke their legs.

65. Jesus.

66. The body of Jesus.

67. Mary Magdalene.

68. She ran to Simon Peter and other disciples.

69. "Two angels in white sitting, the one at the head, and the other at the feet, where the body of Jesus had lain."

70. "...Peace be unto you."

71. Thomas.

72. "My Lord and my God."

73. Twenty-five.

74. Twenty-one.

75. Acts.

ACTS

ANSWERS:

1. "...and falling headlong, he burst asunder in the midst, and all his bowels gushed out."

2. "The field of blood."

3. "And there appeared unto them cloven tongues like as of fire, and it sat upon each of them."

4. "...dream dreams":

5. "...blood, and fire, and vapour of smoke":

6. Darkness.

7. Blood.

8. "...footstool."

9. "Repent, and be baptized..."

10. The temple.

11. Joseph.

12. Corn.

13. Egypt.

14. "...holy ground."

15. Golden calf.

16. "...Dorcas: this woman was full of good works and almsdeeds which she did."

17. Coats and garments.

18. Peter.

19. "...to pray about the sixth hour":

20. "...Holy Ghost."

21. Sword.

22. "...the angel of the Lord..."

23. "And immediately the angel of the Lord smote him, because he gave not God the glory:..."

24. "...he was eaten of worms, and gave up the ghost."

25. Seven nations.

26. The magistrates had them strip of their clothing and then ordered them to be beaten and put in prison.

27. Jews.

28. "And suddenly there was a great earthquake, so that the foundations of the prison were shaken: and immediately all the doors were opened, and every one's bands were loosed."

29. "...Believe on the Lord Jesus Christ, and thou shalt be saved...."

30. "TO THE UNKNOWN GOD."

31. "...repent."

32. Jesus.

33. "...speak, and hold not they peace":

34. "...It is more blessed to give than to receive."

35. Seven, all four daughters were virgins.

36. Two chains.

37. Spirit and angel.

38. Nazarene.

39. "...just and unjust."

40. "....I am Jesus whom thou persecutest."

41. "...Paul, thou art beside thyself; much learning doth make thee mad."

42. Italy.

43. "Julius a centurion of Augustus."

44. They all escaped and swam to land.

45. The island of Melita.

46. A viper.

47. "And he shook off the beast into the fire, and felt no harm."

48. "Paul dwelt two whole years in his own hired house."

49. Twenty-eight.

50. Romans.

ROMANS

ANSWERS:

1. "...Greek."
2. "...The just shall live by faith..."
3. "...fools,"
4. "...reprobate mind..."
5. "...fornication, wickedness, covetousness, maliciousness, full of envy, murder, debate, deceit, malignity, whispers, backbiters, haters of God, despiteful, proud, boasters, inventors of evil things, disobedient to parents,"
6. Chapter three verse ten.
7. "...with their tongues they have used deceit;..."
8. "Whose mouth is full of cursing and bitterness":
9. "...blood":
10. Jews and Gentiles.
11. Abraham.
12. "...Lord Jesus Christ":
13. "...the ungodly."
14. "...died for us."
15. "...death;..."
16. "...but the gift of God is eternal life through Jesus Christ our Lord."
17. God.
18. "...ye shall die:..."
19. "...Abba, Father."
20. "...God, to them who are the called according to his purpose."
21. "...be against us."
22. "...tribulation, or distress, or persecution, or famine, or nakedness, or peril, or sword?"
23. "...death, nor life, nor angels, nor principalities, nor powers, nor things present, nor things to come, nor height, nor depth, nor any other creature..."
24. "...younger."
25. Esau.
26. "...clay..."

27. "...believeth."

28. Repentance.

29. "...feed him;...".

30. "...give him drink:..."

31. "...good."

32. "...damnation."

33. "...hath fulfilled the law."

34. "...Thou shalt not commit adultery, Thou shalt not kill, Thou shalt not steal, Thou shalt not bear false witness, Thou shalt not covet;..."

35. "...love thy neighbor as thyself."

36. "...Lord's."

37. "...dead and living."

38. "...Christ."

39. "...righteousness, and peace, and joy in the Holy Ghost."

40. "...weak, and not to please ourselves."

41. Spain.

42. "...of peace be with you all. Amen."

43. "...kiss..."

44. Sixteen.

45. I Corinthians.

I CORINTHIANS

ANSWERS:

1. "...Jesus Christ...."
2. "...Corinth..."
3. "...Lord Jesus Christ."
4. "...power of God."
5. "...meat:..."
6. "...dwelleth in you?"
7. "...destroy; for the temple of God is holy, which temple ye are."
8. "...holy..."
9. "...warn you."
10. "...power."
11. "Know ye not that the unrighteous shall not inherit the kingdom of God? Be not deceived: neither fornicators, nor idolaters, nor adulterers, nor effeminate, nor abusers of themselves with mankind, Nor thieves, nor covetous, nor drunkards, nor revilers, nor extortioners, shall inherit the kingdom of God."
12. "...body, and in your spirit, which are God's."
13. "...his own wife..."
14. "...her own husband."
15. Christ.
16. "...evil things..."
17. "...devils, and not to God: and I would not that ye should have fellowship with devils."
18. "...man."
19. The man.
20. "...if a man have long hair, it is a shame unto him?"
21. "...glory to her: for her hair is given her for a covering."
22. Word of wisdom, word of knowledge, faith, gifts of healing, miracles, prophecy, discerning of spirits, divers kinds of tongues, and interpretation of tongues.
23. "...charity."
24. Men, beasts, fishes, and birds.
25. The sun, moon, and stars.
26. The natural body, and the spiritual body.
27. "...holy kiss."
28. "...Christ Jesus. Amen."
29. Sixteen.
30. II Corinthians.

II CORINTHIANS

ANSWERS:

1. "...from the Lord Jesus Christ."

2. "...God..."

3. "...sight:)"

4. Joining together.

5. "...for God loveth a cheerful giver."

6. "...weighty and powerful; but his bodily presence is weak, and his speech contemptible."

7. "...in perils of waters, in perils of robbers, in perils by mine own countrymen, in perils by the heathen, in perils in the city, in perils in the wilderness, in perils in the sea, in perils among false brethren;..."

8. "In weariness and painfulness, in watchings often, hunger and thirst, in fastings often, in cold and nakedness."

9. "...kiss."

10. "...salute you."

11. Thirteen.

12. The book of Galations.

GALATIANS

ANSWERS:

1. Yes.

2. "...accursed."

3. "...faith."

4. the law.

5. "...neighbour as thyself."

6. Yes.

7. "...the kingdom of God."

8. "...love, joy, peace, longsuffering, gentleness, goodness, faith, Meekness, temperance":

9. "...walk in the Spirit."

10. "...deceiveth himself."

11. "...corruption..."

12. Six.

13. Ephesians.

EPHESIANS

ANSWERS:

1. "...feet..."
2. "...church."
3. "...faith; and that not of yourselves: it is the gift of God."
4. Jesus Christ.
5. God.
6. "...Father of our Lord Jesus Christ."
7. "...children."
8. "...word of God":
9. "...Lord Jesus Christ in sincerity. Amen."
10. Six.
11. Phillipians.

PHILIPPIANS

ANSWERS:

1. "...gain."

2. "...others."

3. Knee, heaven, earth, earth.

4. "And that every tongue should confess that Jesus Christ is Lord, to the glory of God the Father."

5. Dogs, evil workers, concision.

6. "Rejoice in the Lord always: and again I say, Rejoice."

7. "...all men. The Lord is at hand."

8. True, honest, just, pure, lovely, good report.

9. "...Christ which strengtheneth me."

10. "The grace of our Lord Jesus Christ be with you all. Amen."

11. Four.

12. Colossians.

COLOSSIANS

ANSWERS:

1. "...Jesus Christ, by the will of God, and Timotheus our brother,"

2. "...and hath translated us into the kingdom of his dear Son":

3. "...the firstborn of every creature":

4. The church.

5. "...spirit, joying and beholding your order, and the stedfastness of your faith in Christ."

6. "...walk ye in him":

7. "...earth."

8. "...also appear with him in glory."

9. "...fornication, uncleanness, inordinate affection, evil concupiscence, and covetousness, which is idolatry":

10. "...anger, wrath, malice, blasphemy, filthy communication out of your mouth."

11. Charity.

12. "...Lord Jesus, giving thanks to God and the Father by him."

13. Submit.

14. Love.

15. "...obey your parents in all things: for this is well pleasing unto the Lord."

16. "...Grace be with you. Amen."

17. Four.

18. Thessalonians.

I THESSALONIANS

ANSWERS:

1. God.

2. "...Lord."

3. "Now God himself and our Father, and our Lord Jesus Christ, direct our way unto you."

4. "...holiness."

5. "...rise first":

6. "...thief in the night."

7. "...obtain salvation by our Lord Jesus Christ."

8. 16 Rejoice evermore.

    17 Pray without ceasing.

    18 In every thing give thanks: for this is the will of God in Christ Jesus concerning you.

    19 Quench not the Spirit.

    20 Despise not prophesyings.

    21 Prove all things; hold fast that which is good.

    22 Abstain from all appearances of evil.

9. Five.

10. II Thessalonians.

II THESSALONIANS

ANSWERS:

1. "...work: only he who now letteth will let, until he be taken out of the way."

2. Traditions.

3. "...word and work."

4. "...faith."

5. "...eat."

6. "...The Lord be with you all."

7. Three.

8. I Timothy.

I TIMOTHY

ANSWERS:

1. "...conscience, and of faith unfeigned":
2. "...lawless and disobedient, for the ungodly and for sinners, for unholy and profane, for murderers of fathers and murderers of mothers, for manslayers, For whoremongers, for them that defile themselves with mankind, for menstealers, for liars, for perjured persons, and if there be any other thing that is contrary to sound doctrine";
3. Sinners.
4. "...the man Christ Jesus";
5. "...holy hands, without wrath and doubting."
6. Appear "...not with broided hair, or gold, or pearls, or costly array."
7. Adam.
8. "...a pure conscience."
9. "...God was manifest in the flesh, justified in the Spirit, seen of angels, preached unto the Gentiles, believed on in the world, received up into glory."
10. "Let no man despise thy youth; but be thou an example of the believers, in word, in conversation, in charity, in spirit, in faith, in purity."
11. "...pure."
12. "...stomach's sake and thine often infirmities."
13. "...carry nothing out."
14. "...evil..."
15. "...righteousness, godliness, faith, love, patience, meekness."
16. Six.
17. II Timothy.

II TIMOTHY

ANSWERS:

1. "...God, according to the promise of life which is in Christ Jesus,"
2. Power, love, and a sound mind.
3. "...dead with him, we shall also live with him":
4. Gold, silver, wood, earth.
5. Perilous.
6. "For men shall be lovers of their own selves, covetous, boasters, proud, blasphemers, disobedient to parents, unthankful, unholy."
7. "...I have kept the faith":
8. "...Grace be with you. Amen."
9. Four.
10. Titus.

TITUS

ANSWERS:

1. "...good men, sober, just, holy, temperate";
2. "...masters,..."
3. "...foolish, disobedient, deceived, serving divers lusts and pleasures, living in malice and envy, hateful, and hating one another."
4. Cretians.
5. Three.
6. Philemon.

PHILEMON

ANSWERS:

1. "...Lord Jesus, and toward all saints";
2. "...on mine account."
3. One.
4. Hebrews.

HEBREWS

ANSWERS:

1. "...fire."

2. "...iniquity..." (sin)

3. "...the earth..."

4. "...God."

5. "...sin."

6. "...Christ,...".

7. Seventh.

8. Harden.

9. "...twoedged sword, piercing even to the dividing asunder of soul and spirit, and of the joints and marrow, and is a discerner of the thoughts and intents of the heart."

10. "...Holiest of all";

11. Bulls and goats.

12. "...a good report."

13. Isaac.

14. Offer Isaac as a sacrifice to the Lord. Abraham was going to kill him by stabbing him and then burning him on an altar he had made.

15. The sons of Joseph.

16. "...Israel; and gave commandment concerning his bones."

17. Pharaoh's daughter.

18. Egyptians.

19. Jericho.

20. "...bastards, and not sons."

21. Esau.

22. "...fire."

23. Whoremongers, adulterers.

24. Italy.

25. Thirteen.

26. James.

JAMES

ANSWERS:

1. "...God and of the Lord Jesus Christ..."

2. "...worketh patience."

3. "...because as the flower of the grass he shall pass away."

4. Goodly, vile.

5. "...horses' mouths,..."

6. "...that they may obey us; and we turn about their whole body."

7. "...it is an unruly evil, full of deadly poison."

8. "...God."

9. God, devil.

10. "...lift you up."

11. "...vapour, that appeareth for a little time, and then vanisheth away."

12. Corrupted, motheaten.

13. "...be a witness against you, and shall eat your flesh as it were fire. Ye have heaped treasure together for the last days."

14. Patient, hearts, Lord.

15. Elias.

16. "...and the heaven gave rain, and the earth brought forth her fruit."

17. "...save a soul from death, and shall hide a multitude of sins."

18. Five.

19. The book of I Peter

I PETER

ANSWERS:

1. Yes.

2. Gold.

3. "...silver and gold, from your vain conversation received by tradition from your fathers."

4. "...blemish and without spot":

5. "...grass..."

6. "...the flower of grass. The grass withereth, and the flower thereof falleth away":

7. "...for ever..."

8. "...righteous..."

9. "...evil."

10. Eight.

11. "...right hand of God; angels and authorities and powers being made subject unto him."

12. Charity, multitude, sins.

13. "...crown of glory that fadeth not away."

14. Proud, humble.

15. God.

16. The devil.

17. Five.

18. II Peter.

II PETER

ANSWERS:

1. Into hell.

2. "...judgement";

3. "...righteousness..."

4. God burned them up into ashes.

5. 1000 years. "...that one day is with the Lord as a thousand years, and a thousand years as one day."

6. Thief.

7. "...the heavens shall pass away with a great noise, and the elements shall melt with fervent heat..."

8. It will burn up.

9. Three.

10. I John.

I JOHN

ANSWERS:

1. "...ourselves, and the truth is not in us."

2. "...abideth for ever."

3. He killed his brother.

4. "...deed and in truth."

5. "...love."

6. No. "If we love one another, God dwelleth in us..."

7. "We love him, because he first loved us."

8. "...liar: for he that loveth not his brother whom he hath seen, how can he love God whom he hath not seen?"

9. "...the Father, the Word, and the Holy Ghost: and these three are one."

10. "...the spirit, and the water, and the blood: and these three agree in one."

11. "...sin: and there is a sin not unto death."

12. "...idols. Amen."

13. Five.

14. II John.

II JOHN

ANSWERS:

1. Deceiver, antichrist.
2. "...full reward."
3. "...Father and the Son."
4. One.
5. III John.

III JOHN

ANSWERS:

1. "...good..."
2. Good, evil.
3. One.
4. Jude.

JUDE

ANSWERS:

1. Jesus Christ.
2. James.
3. "...ten thousands of his saints,"
4. One.
5. The book of Revelation.

REVELATION

ANSWERS:

1. Seven.

2. Beginning and end.

3. "...seven churches which are in Asia;..."

4. Seven.

5. "His head and his hairs were white like wool, as white as snow;..."

6. "And his feet like unto fine brass, as if they burned in a furnace;..."

7. "...and his voice as the sound of many waters."

8. A twoedged sword.

9. "...Fear not; I am the first and the last";

10. Jesus.

11. One with two edges.

12. Come unto thee quickly.

13. Let him hear, hidden manna, white stone.

14. A prophetess.

15. No.

16. "And I will kill her children with death; and all the churches shall know that I am he which searcheth the reins and hearts: and I will give unto every one of you according to your works."

17. Philadelphia.

18. "...shut it: for thou hast a little strength, and hast kept my word, and hast not denied my name."

19. Jerusalem.

20. "...cold nor hot..."

21. "...come in to him, and will sup with him, and he with me."

22. "...four and twenty elders sitting, clothed in white raiment; and they had on their heads crowns of gold."

23. "And out of the throne proceeded lightnings and thunderings and voices:..."

24. "...and there were seven lamps of fire burning before the throne, which are the seven Spirits of God."

25. A lion, calf, man, eagle.

26. "...Holy, holy, holy, Lord God Almighty, which was, and is, and is to come."

27. Seven.

28. White.

29. Red.

30. Black.

31. Pale.

32. "...and his name that sat on him was Death, and Hell followed him..."

33. "...I saw under the altar the souls of them that were slain for the word of God, and for the testimony which they held":

34. "...and, lo, there was a great earthquake; and the sun became black as sackcloth of hair, and the moon became as blood."

35. "...throne, and unto the Lamb."

36. Feed, lead.

37. "...silence in heaven about the space of half an hour."

38. A golden altar.

39. "...hail and fire mingled with blood..."

40. "...the sea: and the third part of the sea became blood";

41. Wormwood, wormwood.

42. "...and I saw a star fall from heaven unto the earth: and to him was given the key of the bottomless pit."

43. "...like unto horses prepared unto battle; and on their heads were as it were crowns like gold, and their faces were as the faces of men."

44. 7,000 people.

45. Sun, moon, twelve stars.

46. "...seven heads and ten horns, and seven crowns upon his heads."

47. Go into captivity, killed with the sword.

48. "...keep the commandments of God, and the faith of Jesus."

49. "...seven last plagues; for in them is filled up the wrath of God."

50. "...clothed in pure and white linen, and having their breasts girded with golden girdles."

51. "...Armageddon."

52. "...blasphemed God because of the plague of the hail; for the plague thereof was exceeding great."

53. Seven, five, one.

54. "...Alleluia; Salvation, and glory, and honour, and power, unto the Lord our God":

55. Faithful and True.

56. "...The Word of God."

57. "...KING OF KINGS, AND LORD OF LORDS."

58. An angel.

59. 1,000 years.

60. They will be beheaded.

61. "...and they lived and reigned with Christ a thousand years."

62. He will be released from the bottomless pit.

63. Satan will deceive them.

64. "...lake of fire and brimstone, where the beast and the false prophet are and shall be tormented day and night for ever and ever."

65. To the lake of fire.

66. New Jerusalem.

67. Alpha, Omega, beginning, end.

68. "...twelve gates..."

69. Twelve.

70. "...blessed is he that keepeth the sayings of the prophecy of this book."

71. "...that they may have right to the tree of life, and may enter in through the gates into the city."

72. "...add unto him the plagues that are written in this book":

73. "...take away his part out of the book of life, and out of the holy city, and from the things which are written in this book."

74. "...Surely I come quickly...."

75. "The grace of our Lord Jesus Christ be with you all. Amen."

76. Twenty-two.

QUESTIONS FROM THE BIBLE:

1. What town did Mary, the mother of Jesus, live in?
2. Who was Mary's husband?
3. Who were Joseph and Mary descents of?
4. Who was the angel that told Mary she would be the mother of Jesus?
5. When Pontius Pilate asked the crowd if they wanted Jesus or the murderer released, who did they choose? What was his name?
6. What did the soldiers place on Jesus' head before he died on the cross?
7. In what town did Jesus cure the ten lepers?
8. Jesus said, "Suffer the little children to come unto me, and forbid them not: for of such is the ..." what?
9. Lazarus had two sisters. What were their names?
10. What is the parable of the Good Samaritan?
11. How old was Jesus when he went with his parents to Jerusalem to celebrate the feast of the Pasch?
12. What presents did the wise men bring to Baby Jesus?
13. What does the present gold stand for?
14. What does myrrh stand for?
15. What does frankincense stand for?
16. How old was Aaron when he died?
17. How many children did Aaron and his wife have?
18. Where did Aaron die?
19. What well-known man in the Bible lived like a hermit?
20. When John the Baptist came out of his life style as a hermit, what did he preach was coming?
21. Where did Jesus preach the Sermon on the Mount?
22. Who ordered John the Baptist to be decapitated?
23. Who was Jesus talking to when he said, "...upon this rock I will build my church; and the gates of hell shall not prevail against it"?
24. What is the meaning of a rainbow?
25. In what book of the New Testament does it tell us when the Ascension took place?
26. When Jesus kicked over the tables in the temple and threw out the moneychangers, he said, "My house should..."what?

27. There are at least 16 women in the Old Testament. Name ten of them.

28. There are three Mary's in the New Testament. Who are they?

29. What was Ruth's color of hair?

30. How long was Ruth married?

31. What was Ruth's husband's name?

32. Who was Ruth's mother-in-law?

33. Ruth had a son. What was his name?

34. There were three important cities in the Roman Empire. Name two of them.

35. What is the third commandment?

36. What is the sixth commandment?

37. What is the eighth commandment?

38. Who was Leah's sister?

39. Jericho is in what country?

40. In what chapter of Matthew tells us about the second coming and the destruction of the temple of Jerusalem?

41. What is the great commandment from God that we should use to direct our lives?

42. In what book is the creation story?

43. In what book is the birth of Christ?

44. In what book are the Ten Commandments?

45. In what book is the Sermon on the Mount?

46. In what book is the Lord's Prayer?

47. In what book is the Prodigal Son?

48. In what books is the Death of Christ?

49. In what book is the great flood?

50. In what books is the Resurrection of Christ?

51. In what book is the Ascension?

52. Who wrote the Old Testament?

53. Who wrote the New Testament?

54. How many books are there in the Old Testament?

55. How many books are in the New Testament?

56. What is the longest book in the Bible?

ANSWERS:

1. Nazareth.
2. Joseph.
3. King David.
4. Gabriel.
5. The murderer, Barabbas.
6. A crown of thorns.
7. Galilee.
8. "...kingdom of God."
9. Mary and Martha.
10. Love your neighbor.
11. 12 years old.
12. Frankincense, myrrh, and gold.
13. King.
14. That Jesus is man as well as God.
15. This Child is God.
16. 123 years old.
17. Four sons.
18. On Mount Hor.
19. John the Baptist.
20. The coming of Christ.
21. Capernaum, a little town by the sea of Galilee.
22. King Herod.
23. Peter.
24. It is God's promise that he will never again flood the earth.
25. Luke chapter 24.
26. "...be a house of prayer, but you have made it a den of thieves."
27. Miriam, Rachel, Eve, Esther, Ruth, Leah, Sarah, Deborah, Hagar, Lot's wife—Dinah, Rebekah, Jochebed, Rahab, Naomi, and Hannah.
28. Mary the Mother of Jesus, Mary of Bethany, and Mary Magdalene.

29. Red.

30. Ten years.

31. Mahlon.

32. Naomi.

33. Obed.

34. Ephesus, Rome, Corinth.

35. "Remember the sabbath day, to keep it holy."

36. "Thou shalt not commit adultery."

37. "Thou shalt not bear false witness against thy neighbor."

38. Rachel.

39. Canaan.

40. The twenty-fourth chapter of Matthew.

41. He said "And thou shalt love the Lord thy God with all thine heart, and with all thy soul, and with all thy might."

42. Genesis.

43. Matthew and Luke.

44. Exodus.

45. Matthew.

46. Luke.

47. Luke.

48. Luke and John.

49. Genesis.

50. Matthew, Luke, and John.

51. Acts.

52. Moses and the Prophets.

53. The Evangelists and the Apostles.

54. Thirty-nine.

55. Twenty-seven.

56. Psalms.

*The author begs the reader's understanding that this book is not in any way meant to take anything away from the Word of God, the Bible. If something has been inadvertently left out or written incorrectly, which is different from the Kings James Bible, it was a mistake. There was never an intent to detract anything from the Bible. Thank you for your understanding.